D1008748

Index to

OPERA, OPERETTA AND
MUSICAL COMEDY SYNOPSES

in Collections and Periodicals

by

Jeanette Marie Drone

The Scarecrow Press, Inc.
Metuchen, N.J. & London
1978

Library of Congress Cataloging in Publication Data

Drone, Jeanette Marie, 1940-
    Index to opera, operetta, and musical comedy
synopses in collections and periodicals.

    1. Operas--Stories, plots, etc.--Indexes.
2. Musical revues, comedies, etc.--Stories, plots,
etc. Indexes. I. Title.
ML128.04D76   016.7821'3   77-25822
ISBN 0-8108-1100-6

PREFACE

This project was started as a result of spending many hours searching for a specific opera synopsis. While searching Cumulative Book Index, trying to locate an index to synopses, I made a list of collections of stories, plots, etc. which were published after 1926. * By visiting the Library of Congress and with the help of the Memphis State University Libraries Interlibrary Loan Department, I was able to locate the collections indexed in this publication. The decision to include periodical titles came much later, and therefore I have been limited to the sources readily at hand. I am planning to continue the project, and hope that future supplements or editions will contain increased coverage of periodical literature.

The main objective was to index collections in the English language which contain synopses of operas by various composers. Most of the collections were found in Library of Congress classification numbers MT 95, ML 1905, and ML 1711. Collections of synopses of the works of one or two specific composers were not included since these collections can readily be found by using the card catalog, and are generally classified in MT 100. An exception was made for Bierley, Paul E., John Philip Sousa; a descriptive catalog of his works.

---

*A source indexing collections before this date is: Rieck, Waldemar. Opera plots; an index to the stories of operas, operettas, ballets, etc., from the sixteenth to the twentieth century. N.Y.: New York Public Library, 1927.

iii

The manner in which this source is classified does not lend itself to being recognized as a source of synopses. Dictionaries and encyclopedias of opera, most generally classified in ML 102, are not included. A bibliography of sources of synopses of the works of individual composers (including biographies) and dictionaries containing synopses appears at the end of this book.

Index to Opera, Operetta, and Musical Comedy Synopses... is an index to 74 collections and four periodical titles. It includes 1,605 titles by 627 composers, with 414 title cross-references. The index is arranged in four sections: 1) a list of collections and periodicals indexed, coded by number (collections) and letters (periodicals); 2) an index by title of opera, operetta, and musical comedy arranged alphabetically with code numbers for location; 3) a composer index; 4) a bibliography of dictionaries with synopses, and additional sources with synopses of the operas, operettas, and musical comedies of individual composers.

No attempt is made to put titles in their original language. Appropriate "see" references are made for titles in other languages, popular titles, and/or subtitles. To conserve space, all initial articles in the titles are omitted. Initials are filed at the beginning of their respective letters. "Mr." is interfiled with "Mister." Appropriate "see" references are used for words that are frequently abbreviated and for composer names with prefixes.

Entries from Opera News refer to the sections devoted to the opera broadcast of the week and page numbers are not included. However, if a synopsis appears even though the opera is not the broadcast of the week, then page numbers are included.

CONTENTS

PART I

Collections and Periodicals Indexed

COLLECTIONS INDEXED

01 Annesley, Charles. Homebook of the opera; including the standard operaglass. New York: Dial
   Press, Inc., 1938.

02 Annesley, Charles. The standard operaglass. New
   York: Brentano's, 1899.

03 Biancolli, Louis, comp. The opera reader. New
   York: McGraw-Hill, 1953.

04 Biancolli, Louis, and Bagar, Robert. The Victor
   book of operas. New York: Simon and Schuster,
   1949.

05 Bierley, Paul E. John Philip Sousa; a descriptive
   catalog of his works. Urbana: University of
   Illinois Press, 1973.

06 Bradford, Reuben A. Opera, once over lightly.
   New York: Perennial Press, 1955.

07 Brook, Donald. Companion to opera. London:
   Rockliff, 1947.

08 Bulla, Clyde Robert. More stories of favorite
   operas. New York: Thomas Y. Crowell, 1965.

09 Bulla, Clyde Robert. Stories of favorite operas.
   New York: Thomas Y. Crowell, 1959.

10 Carlsen, Irna M. Russian opera reader. Vancou-
   ver, B.C., 1957.

3

4 Collections Indexed

11 Crosland, Margaret. Home book of operas. London: Arco Publishers, 1957.

12 Cross, Milton. Complete stories of the great operas. Garden City, N.Y.: Doubleday, 1947.

13 Cross, Milton, and Kohrs, Karl. More stories of the great operas. Garden City, N.Y.: Doubleday, 1971.

14 Cross, Milton, and Kohrs, Karl, eds. The new Milton Cross' complete stories of the great operas. Rev. & enl. ed. Garden City, N.Y.: Doubleday, 1955.

15 Davidson, Gladys. Barnes book of the opera. New York: A. S. Barnes, 1962. (New printing, 1975)

16 Davidson, Gladys. Modern opera stories. London: Werner Laurie, 1956.

17 Davidson, Gladys. New stories of grand opera. London: Werner Laurie, 1958.

18 Davidson, Gladys. Standard stories from the operas. Combined vol. London: Werner Laurie, 1944, 1956.

19 Decca book of opera. London: Werner Laurie, 1956.

20 Dike, Helen. Stories from the great Metropolitan operas. New York: Random House, 1943.

21 Drinkrow, John. The operetta book. New York: Drake Publishers, Inc., 1973.

Drinkrow, John. The vintage operetta book. Reading: Osprey, 1972. (See no. 21)

22 Drinkrow, John. The vintage musical comedy book. Reading: Osprey, 1974.

23 Drummond, Andrew H. American opera librettos.
    Metuchen, N.J.: Scarecrow Press, 1973.

24 Eaton, Quaintance. Opera production; a handbook.
    Minneapolis: University of Minnesota Press,
    1961.

25 Eaton, Quaintance. Opera production II; a hand-
    book. Minneapolis: University of Minnesota
    Press, 1974.

26 England, Paul. Favorite operas by German and
    French composers. New York: Dover Publica-
    tions, 1973.

27 England, Paul. Favorite operas by Italian and
    French composers. New York: Dover Publica-
    tions, 1973.

    England, Paul. Fifty favorite operas. 2nd ed.
    London: George G. Harrap, 1929. (See nos.
    26, 27, 72)

28 Ewen, David. The book of European light opera.
    New York: Holt, Rinehart, & Winston, 1962.

29 Ewen, David. New complete book of the American
    musical theatre. New York: Holt, Rinehart &
    Winston, 1959, 1970.

30 Fellner, Rudolph. Opera themes and plots. New
    York: Simon and Schuster, 1958.

31 Holde, Arthur. A treasury of the great operas.
    New York: Bantam Books, 1965.

32 Howard, John Tasker. The world's great operas.
    New York: Grosset & Dunlap, 1948.

33 Howard, John Tasker. The world's great operas.
    Rev. ed. New York: Modern Library, 1959.

34 Hubbard, William Lines, ed. American history

and encyclopedia of music. 2 v. New York:
Irving Square, 1910.

35 Jacobs, Arthur, and Sadie, Stanley. Great operas
    in synopsis. New York: Thomas Y. Crowell
    Co., 1966.

36 Jacobs, Arthur, and Sadie, Stanley. Opera, a
    modern guide. New York: Drake Publishers,
    1972.

37 Jacobs, Arthur, and Sadie, Stanley. The opera
    guide. London: Hamish Hamilton, 1964.

    Jacobs, Arthur, and Sadie, Stanley. The Pan book
    of opera. (See no. 37)

38 Kaufmann, Helen, and Simon, Henry. Five famous
    operas and their backgrounds. Garden City,
    N. Y.: Doubleday, 1973.

39 Kaufmann, Helen. Stories of one hundred operas.
    New York: Grosset & Dunlap, 1960.

40 Kobbe, Gustav. Kobbe's complete opera book.
    Ed. & rev. ed. New York: G. P. Putnam's
    Sons, 1972.

41 Lubbock, Mark. Complete book of light opera.
    New York: Appleton-Century-Crofts, 1962.

42 McSpadden, J. Walker. Opera and musical come-
    dies. Enl. ed. New York: Thomas Y. Cro-
    well, 1951.

43 McSpadden, J. Walker. Stories from the great
    operas. New York: Thomas Y. Crowell, 1923.

44 Marek, George. Opera as theater. New York:
    Harper and Row, 1962.

45 Martin, George. The opera companion, a guide for
    the casual opera goer. Vol. 2: Synopses. New
    York: Dodd, Mead & Co., 1961.

46 Matthews, Thomas. Stories of the world's great
    operas. New York: Golden Press, 1968.

47 Milligan, Harold Vincent. Stories of famous operas.
    New York: Permabooks, 1950.

48 Moore, Frank Ledlie, comp. Crowell's handbook
    of world opera. New York: Thomas Y. Cro-
    well, 1961.

49 Morley, Sir Alexander F. The Harrap opera guide.
    London: George Harrap & Co., 1970.

50 Newman, Ernest. Great operas. 2 vols. New
    York: Vintage Books, 1958.

51 Newman, Ernest. More stories of famous operas.
    New York: Alfred A. Knopf, 1943.

    Newman, Ernest. Opera night. London: Putnam,
    1943, 1944. (See no. 51)

52 Newman, Ernest. Seventeen famous operas. New
    York: Alfred A. Knopf, 1955.

53 Newman, Ernest. Stories of great operas: I.
    Richard Wagner. New York: Alfred A. Knopf,
    1931.

54 Newman, Ernest. Stories of great operas: II.
    Mozart to Thomas. New York: Alfred A.
    Knopf, 1929.

55 Newman, Ernest. Stories of great operas: III.
    Verdi to Puccini. New York: Alfred A. Knopf,
    1930.

56 Ordway, Edith B. Fifty-six of the best operas.
    Rev. & enl. ed. New York: A. L. Burt, Co.,
    1932.

57 Peltz, Mary Ellis. Introduction to opera. New
    York: Barnes & Noble, 1956.

58 Peltz, Mary Ellis. Introduction to opera. 2nd ed.
    New York: Barnes and Noble, 1962.

59 Peltz, Mary Ellis. Opera lover's companion. Chi-
    cago: Ziff-Davis Publishing Co., 1948.

60 Sanborn, Pitts. The Metropolitan book of the opera.
    New York: Garden City Publishing, 1942.

61 Simon, Henry W. Festival of opera. Garden City,
    N. Y.: Hanover House, 1957.

62 Simon, Henry W. One hundred great operas and
    their stories. Garden City, N. Y.: Doubleday,
    1957, 1960.

63 Simon, Henry W., ed. A treasury of grand opera.
    New York: Simon and Schuster, 1946.

64 Thompson, Oscar, ed. Plots of the operas. Cleve-
    land: World Publishing Co., 1943.

65 Tumbusch, Tom. Theatre student guide to Broad-
    way musical theatre. New York: Rosen Press,
    1972.

66 Upton, George P., and Browski, Felix. The
    standard opera guide. Garden City, N. Y.:
    Halcyon House, 1947.

67 Victor book of the opera. 13th ed. Rev. by Henry
    W. Simon. New York: Simon and Schuster,
    1968.

68 Victrola book of the opera. 7th ed. Rev. Camden,
    N. J.: Victor Talking Machine Co., 1924.

69 Westerman, Gerhart von. Opera guide. London:
    Sphere Books, 1968.

70 Williams, Stephen. Come to the opera. Green-
    wich, Conn.: Fawcett Publications, 1961.

71 Blythe, Ronald, ed. Aldeburgh anthology. Alde-
    burgh, Suffolk: Snape Maltings Foundation, Ltd.
    [Distributed by] London: Faber Music Ltd.,
    1972.

72 England, Paul. Favorite operas by German and
    Russian composers. New York: Dover Publica-
    tions, 1973.

73 Teasdale, May Silva. [Handbook of] 20th century
    opera at home and abroad; 1900 through season
    1937-1938. New York: E. P. Dutton & Co.,
    1938. (Reprint: New York: Da Capo, 1976)

74 Kobbe, Gustave. The new Kobbe's complete opera
    book. Ed. and rev. by The Earl of Harewood.
    New York: G. P. Putnam's, 1976.

                    PERIODICALS INDEXED

JAMS   Journal of the American Musicological Society.
          Vols. 1-28, 1948-1976.

MT   Musical Times. Vols. 112-116, 1971-1975.

NY   The New Yorker. 1976-

ON   Opera News. Vols. 14-40, 1949-1976.

PART II

Title Index
with Location Codes

A BASSO PORTO (Spinelli) 64

ABANDONMENT OF ARIADNE see TROIS OPERAS-
MINUTES

ABARIS, OU LES BOREADES (Rameau) MT 116
#1586 p. 327

ABDUCTION FROM THE SERAGLIO (Mozart) 01, 02,
03, 04, 11, 12, 14, 15, 18, 19, 24, 26, 28, 32, 33,
35, 36, 37, 39, 40, 42, 45, 48, 49, 50, 51, 56, 60,
61, 62, 64, 67, 69, 70, 72, 73, 74

ABDUCTION OF EUROPA see TROIS OPERAS-
MINUTES

ABU HASSAN (Weber) 01, 02, 24, 28, 69

ACIS AND GALATEA (Handel) 24, 69, 71

ADRIANA LECOUVREUR (Cilea) 13, 19, 25, 34, 40,
48, 61, 64, 67, 73, 74; ON 27 #14; ON 30 #14; ON
33 #25

ADVENTURES OF MR. BROUCEK see EXCURSIONS
OF MR. BROUCEK

AEGYPTISCHE HELENA see EGYPTIAN HELEN

AFRICAINE (Meyerbeer) 01, 02, 03, 04, 12, 14, 15,
17, 19, 25, 32, 33, 34, 40, 42, 48, 60, 61, 62, 64,
66, 68, 69, 74

13

AFRICAN MAID see AFRICAINE

AGAMEMNON (Hamilton) 25

AIDA (Verdi) 01, 02, 03, 04, 06, 07, 09, 11, 12, 14, 15, 18, 19, 20, 24, 27, 30, 31, 32, 33, 34, 35, 36, 37, 38, 39, 40, 42, 43, 45, 46, 47, 48, 49, 50, 52, 55, 56, 57, 58, 60, 61, 62, 63, 64, 66, 67, 68, 69, 70, 73, 74; ON 14 #19; ON 16 #18; ON 17 #12; ON 18 #15; ON 20 #8; ON 21 #15; ON 22 #4; ON 24 #4; ON 26 #16; ON 27 #6; ON 28 #4; ON 29 #19; ON 30 #15; ON 31 #18; ON 32 #12; ON 35 #8-9; ON 37 #16; ON 40 #17

ALAHOR IN GRANATA (Donizetti) JAMS 25 p. 246

ALBERT HERRING (Britten) 11, 15, 16, 24, 40, 42, 45, 48, 49, 69, 71, 74

ALCESTA (Lully) MT 114 #1559 p. 21; MT 114 #1561 p. 296

ALCESTE (Gluck) 03, 04, 15, 17, 19, 24, 32, 33, 39, 40, 48, 49, 61, 62, 64, 67, 69, 74; ON 16 #21; ON 25 #14

ALCHEMIST (Scott) 73

ALCINA (Handel) 25, 35, 36, 37, 69, 74

ALEKO (Rachmaninoff) 10, 15, 18

ALESSANDRO STRADELLA (Flotow) 01, 02, 32, 33, 34, 42, 64, 66, 68

ALFRED (Dvorak) 73

ALKESTIS (Boughton) 15, 18

ALLEGRO (Rodgers, R.) 29, 42, 65

ALT WIEN (Lanner) 28

AMAHL AND THE NIGHT VISITORS (Menotti) 14, 15, 16, 23, 24, 33, 39, 48, 61, 62, 67, 74

AMASIS, AN EGYPTIAN PRINCESS (Faraday) 41

AMELIA GOES TO THE BALL (Menotti) 04, 15, 16, 23, 24, 32, 33, 39, 42, 48, 61, 64, 73, 74

AMERICA see AMERIKA

AMERICAN MAID (Sousa) 05

AMERICA'S SWEETHEART (Rodgers, R.) 29

AMERIKA (Kohs) 25

AMFIPARNASO (Vecchi) 61

AMICO FRITZ (Mascagni) 01, 02, 15, 18, 25, 32, 33, 34, 40, 42, 48, 64, 74

AMNON AND TAMAR (Tal) 25

AMORE DEI TRE RE (Montemezzi) 01, 04, 12, 14, 24, 32, 33, 39, 40, 42, 47, 48, 56, 60, 61, 62, 64, 66, 73, 74

AMORE MEDICO (Wolf-Ferrari) 01, 24, 28, 32, 33, 42, 73

AMOUR A TROIS see TELEPHONE

AMOUR DES TROIS ORANGES see LOVE FOR THREE ORANGES

AND SO TO BED (Ellis) 41

ANDRE CHENIER (Giordano) 01, 04, 08, 12, 14, 15, 18, 19, 24, 32, 33, 39, 40, 42, 48, 56, 60, 61, 62, 64, 66, 67, 68, 69, 70, 73, 74; ON 19 #4; ON 22 #8; ON 24 #21; ON 27 #17

ANDREA DEL SARTO (Lesur) 25

ANDROMACHE (Windt) 73

ANGE DE FEU (Prokofiev) 25, 74

ANGEL OF FIRE see FLAMING ANGEL

ANGELIQUE (Ibert) 24

ANIARA (Blomdahl) 24, 39, 45

ANIMA ALLEGRA (Vittadini) 73

ANIMAL CRACKERS (Ruby) 29

ANNA BOLENA (Donizetti) 13, 15, 17, 24, 74

ANNIE GET YOUR GUN (Berlin) 22, 29, 41, 42, 65

ANTIGONAE (Orff) 25, 48, 69

ANTONY AND CLEOPATRA (Barber) 13; ON 31 #2

ANYONE CAN WHISTLE (Sondheim) 65

ANYTHING GOES (Porter) 22, 29, 41, 65

APHRODITE (Erlanger) 01, 42, 56, 64

APOLLO AND PERSEPHONE (Cockshott) 25

APOTHECARY see SPEZIALE

APPLAUSE (Strouse) 29, 65

APPLE BLOSSOMS (Kreisler) 29

APPLE TREE (Bock) 29, 65

ARABELLA (Strauss, R.) 11, 14, 15, 18, 19, 24, 33,
39, 40, 48, 49, 61, 62, 64, 67, 69, 73, 74; ON 19 #16;
ON 21 #13; ON 25 #11; ON 30 #7

ARBORE DI DIANA (Martín y Soler)   MT 113 #1552 p. 551-3

ARCADIANS (Monckton)   28, 41, 42

ARDEN MUSS STERBEN (Goehr)   25; MT 115 #1576 p. 492

ARIADNE AUF NAXOS (Strauss, R.)   11, 12, 14, 15, 18, 19, 24, 32, 33, 35, 36, 39, 40, 42, 48, 49, 60, 61, 62, 64, 67, 69, 73, 74; ON 27 #15; ON 34 #22; ON 40 #18

ARIANE ET BARBE BLEUE (Dukas)   01, 11, 15, 18, 25, 32, 33, 34, 39, 40, 42, 48, 60, 64, 66, 73, 74

ARIANNA (Monteverdi)   74

ARIODANTE (Handel)   25; MT 115 #1582 p. 1059

ARIZONA LADY (Kálmán)   41

ARLECCHINO (Busoni)   15, 17, 24, 28, 40, 48, 61, 74

ARLESIANA (Cilea)   19, 40, 48

ARMIDA (Dvorak)   25

ARMIDA (Gluck)   01, 02, 04, 07, 15, 17, 24, 32, 33, 42, 60, 64, 66, 73

ARMIDA (Haydn)   25

ARMORER   see   WAFFENSCHMIED

AROLDO (Verdi)   25, 74

ARTISTS AND MODELS (Coots & Romberg)   29

AS THE GIRLS GO (McHugh)   29

AS THOUSANDS CHEER (Berlin)   29, 42

ASSASSINIO NELLA CATTEDRALE (Pizzetti) 24, 45

ASSEDIO DI CORINTO (Rossini) 13, 25; ON 39 #21; ON 40 #11

AT THE BOAR'S HEAD (Holst) 73

ATTAQUE DU MOULIN (Bruneau) 01, 60, 73

ATTILA (Verdi) 25, 74; MT 113 #1556 p. 997; NY 1/10/77 p. 79-80

AUBE ROUGE (Erlanger) 01

AUF HOHEN BEFEHL see BY ORDER OF HIS HIGH-NESS

AUFSTIEG UND FALL DER STADT MAHAGONNY see RISE AND FALL OF THE CITY MAHAGONNY

AUNT CAROLINE'S WILL (Roussel) 24

AZORA (Hadley) 32, 33, 42, 73

-B-

BA-TA-CLAN (Offenbach) 25

BABES IN ARMS (Rodgers, R.) 29

BABES IN TOYLAND (Herbert) 29, 41, 42

BAERENHAEUTER (Wagner, S.) 34

BAJADERE (Kálmán) 41

BAKER STREET (Grudeff & Jessel, R.) 29, 65

BALALAIKA (Posford & Grun) 41

BALD PRIMA DONNA (Kalmanoff) 25

BALLAD OF AGNES BERNAUER see BERNAUERIN

BALLAD OF BABY DOE (Moore) 13, 23, 24, 33, 45, 48, 67; ON 33 #19

BALLET OF THE PRUDISH MAIDENS see BALLO DELLE INGRATE

BALLO DELLE INGRATE (Monteverdi) 71

BALLO IN MASCHERA (Auber) see GUSTAV III

BALLO IN MASCHERA (Verdi) 01, 02, 03, 04, 07, 08, 11, 12, 14, 15, 18, 19, 24, 27, 30, 32, 33, 34, 35, 36, 37, 39, 40, 42, 45, 47, 48, 49, 57, 58, 60, 61, 62, 64, 66, 67, 68, 69, 70, 74; ON 19 #11; ON 20 #5; ON 23 #17; ON 26 #18; ON 27 #10; ON 30 #17; ON 32 #23; ON 35 #14; ON 37 #12; ON 40 #6

BAND WAGON (Schwartz, A.) 29

BANJO EYES (Duke) 29

BARBE-BLEUE (Offenbach) 41, 42

BARBER OF BAGDAD (Cornelius) 01, 02, 19, 24, 28, 32, 33, 34, 40, 42, 48, 51, 60, 64, 69, 74

BARBIERE DI SIVIGLIA (Paisiello) 24, 28

BARBIERE DI SIVIGLIA (Rossini) 01, 02, 03, 04, 06, 07, 09, 11, 12, 14, 15, 18, 19, 20, 24, 27, 28, 30, 31, 32, 33, 34, 35, 36, 37, 39, 40, 42, 45, 46, 47, 48, 49, 50, 52, 54, 56, 57, 58, 60, 61, 62, 64, 66, 67, 68, 69, 70, 74; ON 15 #8; ON 18 #17; ON 19 #7; ON 22 #7; ON 27 #18; ON 30 #20; ON 33 #11; ON 34 #9-10; ON 35 #17; ON 37 #22; ON 38 #17; ON 40 #12

BARRIER (Meyerowitz) 24

BARTERED BRIDE (Smetana) 01, 02, 03, 04, 07, 08, 11, 12, 14, 15, 18, 19, 20, 24, 28, 32, 33, 35, 36, 39, 40, 42, 47, 48, 49, 51, 60, 61, 62, 64, 66, 67, 68, 69, 70, 73, 74

BARTLEBY (Aschaffenburg) 25

BASOCHE (Messager) 41

BASSARIDS (Henze) 25, 74; MT 115 #1580 p. 831-4;
MT 115 #1582 p. 1057

BASTIEN AND BASTIENNE (Mozart) 15, 17, 19, 24,
28, 39, 61, 62, 69

BAT see FLEDERMAUS

BATTAGLIA DI LEGNANO (Verdi) 25, 74

BEACH OF FALESA (Hoddinott) MT 115 #1573 p. 207

BEAR (Walton) 25, 71, 74

BEARSKIN WEAVER see BAERENHAEUTER

BEATRICE (Messager) 25

BEATRICE DI TENDA (Bellini) 25, 74

BEATRICE ET BENEDICT (Berlioz) 01, 25, 28, 40, 42,
48, 74

BEATRIX CENCI (Ginastera) 25

BEAUTIFUL GALATHEA see SCHOENE GALATHEA

BEAUTY AND THE BEAST (Giannini) 24

BEAUTY STONE (Sullivan) 41

BEGGAR STUDENT (Milloecker) 21, 28, 34, 40, 41, 42,
48, 69, 74

BEGGAR'S OPERA (Pepusch) 11, 24, 28, 34, 39, 40,
42, 48, 74

BEGGAR'S OPERA (Pinkham) 25

BELAGERUNGZUSTAND (Kelemen) 25

BELISAIRE (Donizetti) MT 113 #1549 p. 259

BELL OF THE HERMIT see DRAGONS DE VILLARS

BELL TOWER (Křenek) 24

BELLE HELENE (Offenbach) 21, 24, 28, 34, 41, 42, 49, 66, 69, 74

BELLE OF BOHEMIA (Englander & MacConnell) 29

BELLE OF MAYFAIR (Stuart) 42

BELLE OF NEW YORK (Kerker) 22, 29, 41, 42

BELLS ARE RINGING (Styne) 29, 41, 65

BELLS OF CORNEVILLE see CLOCHES DE CORNE-VILLES

BEN FRANKLIN IN PARIS (Sandrich) 65

BENVENUTO CELLINI (Berlioz) 01, 02, 03, 13, 15, 17, 25, 32, 33, 34, 40, 42, 48, 60, 64, 69, 74

BERNAUERIN (Orff) 25

BERTHA (Rorem) 25

BEST FOOT FORWARD (Martin, H. & Blane) 29

BESUCH DER ALTEN DAME (Einem) 25; MT 114 #1565 p. 731

BETHLEHEM (Boughton) 15, 18

BETROGENE CADI see CADI DUPE

BETROTHAL IN A MONASTERY see DUENNA

BETTELSTUDENT see BEGGAR STUDENT

BEWITCHED CHILD see ENFANT ET LES SORTILEGES

BIG BLACK BOX (Morgenstern) 25

BILLEE TAYLOR (Solomon) 34

BILLION DOLLAR BABY (Gould) 29

BILLY BUDD (Britten) 11, 15, 16, 24, 40, 45, 48, 49, 69, 74; ON 16 #9

BIRD DEALER see VOGELHAENDLER

BITTER SWEET (Coward) 22, 28, 41, 42

BLACK CROOK (Operti) 29

BLACK DOMINO see DOMINO NOIR

BLACK FOREST MAID see SCHWARZWALDMAEDEL

BLACK HUSSAR (Milloecker) 34, 42

BLACK WIDOW (Pasatieri) 25

BLACKSMITH OF GHENT see SCHMIED VON GENT

BLAUE MAZUR (Lehár) 41

BLENNERHASSET (Giannini) 24

BLESS THE BRIDE (Ellis) 22, 41

BLOOD WEDDING (Fortner) see BLUTHOCHZEIT

BLOOD WEDDING (Szokolay) 25

BLOOMER GIRL (Arlen) 29, 42, 65

BLOSSOM TIME (Romberg) 29, 41, 42

BLUE FOREST see FORET BLUE

BLUE PARADISE (Romberg) 29

BLUEBEARD'S CASTLE (Bartók) 15, 16, 24, 40, 48,
49, 67, 69, 74; ON 39 #16

BLUEBIRD see OISEAU BLEU

BLUTHOCHZEIT (Fortner) 69

BOATSWAIN'S MATE (Smyth) 07, 15, 18, 40, 42, 48,
64, 74

BOCCACCIO (Suppé) 21, 25, 28, 34, 41, 42, 69, 74

BOCCACCIO'S "NIGHTINGALE" (Trimble) 25

BOHEME (Puccini) 01, 03, 04, 06, 07, 09, 11, 12, 14,
15, 18, 19, 24, 27, 30, 31, 32, 33, 34, 35, 36, 39, 40,
42, 45, 46, 47, 48, 49, 50, 52, 55, 56, 57, 58, 60, 61,
62, 64, 66, 67, 68, 69, 70, 73, 74; ON 14 #21; ON 15
#21; ON 16 #19; ON 17 #8; ON 17 #16; ON 18 #6; ON
19 #20; ON 21 #20; ON 22 #15; ON 25 #18; ON 26 #10;
ON 28 #18; ON 30 #24; ON 31 #15; ON 33 #13; ON 34
#13; ON 35 #19; ON 37 #11; ON 38 #15

BOHEMIAN GIRL (Balfe) 01, 15, 18, 28, 32, 33, 34,
40, 42, 43, 56, 60, 64, 66, 68, 74

BOMARZO (Ginastera) 25, 67, 74

BOMBO (Romberg) 29

BON VOYAGE see GLUECKLICHE REISE

BOOR (Argento) 24

BOOR (Kay) 25

BORIS GODOUNOV (Musorgskii) 01, 03, 04, 06, 07, 08,
10, 11, 12, 14, 15, 18, 19, 24, 26, 30, 31, 32, 33, 35
36, 38, 39, 40, 42, 45, 46, 47, 48, 49, 50, 51, 56, 57,
58, 60, 61, 62, 64, 66, 67, 68, 69, 70, 72, 73, 74; ON
17 #21; ON 18 #16; ON 20 #18; ON 23 # 20; ON 25 #9;
ON 27 #22; ON 39 #12; ON 40 #12

BOSOM OF THERESE see MAMELLES DE TIRESIAS

BOULEVARD SOLITUDE (Henze) 25, 74

BOY FRIEND (Wilson, S.) 65

BOYS FROM SYRACUSE (Rodgers, R.) 29

BOZENA (Straus) 41

BRANDENBURGERS IN BOHEMIA (Smetana) 25

BRANIBOŘI V CECHACH see BRANDENBURGERS IN
BOHEMIA

BREBIS EGAREE (Milhaud) 73

BRIDE-ELECT (Sousa) 05, 42

BRIEF LIFE see VIDA BREVE

BRIGADOON (Loewe) 22, 29, 41, 42, 65

BRIGANDS (Offenbach) 41, 42

BRONWEN (Holbrooke) 15, 18

BROOK (Salsbury) 29

BROTHER DEVIL see FRA DIAVOLA

BROTHER IN LOVE see FRATE INNAMORATA

BROUCEK'S EXCURSIONS see EXCURSIONS OF MR.
BROUCEK

BRUDER STRAUBINGER (Eysler) 28, 41

BRUTE (Moss) 25

BUFFONATA (Killmayer) 25

BUFFOONERY see BUFFONATA

BUN IS BUNHODES see CRIME AND PUNISHMENT

BUONA FIGLIUOLA (Piccinni) 28

BURGOMASTER (Luders) 42

BURGSCHAFT (Weill) 73

BURNING FIERY FURNACE (Britten) 25, 71, 74

BURNING HOUSE (Hovhannes) 25

BURROW see SUFFICIENT BEAUTY

BUTTERFLY THAT STAMPED see SOLOMON AND
BALKIS

BUTTERFLY WIDOW see WITWE DES SCHMETTER-
LINGS

BY JUPITER (Rodgers, R.) 29

BY ORDER OF HIS HIGHNESS (Reinecke) 02

BY THE BEAUTIFUL SEA (Schwartz, A.) 29

BYE BYE BIRDIE (Strouse) 29, 41, 65

-C-

CABARET (Kander) 29, 65

CABIN IN THE SKY (Duke) 29, 41

CADI DUPE (Gluck) 25, 28

CAGLIOSTRO IN WIEN (Strauss, J.) 21, 28, 41

CALAMITY JANE (Fain) 65

CALIPH OF BAGDAD (Boieldieu) 28

CARDILLAC (Hindemith)   25, 48, 60, 64, 69, 74

CARLO BROSCHI (Auber)   01, 02

CARMEN (Bizet)   01, 02, 03, 04, 06, 07, 09, 11, 12, 14, 15, 18, 19, 20, 24, 27, 30, 31, 32, 33, 34, 35, 36, 38, 39, 40, 42, 43, 44, 45, 46, 47, 48, 49, 50, 52 55, 56, 57, 58, 60, 61, 62, 63, 64, 66, 67, 68, 69, 70, 74; ON 14 #14; ON 16 #15; ON 17 #13; ON 18 #21; ON 19 #13; ON 20 #11; ON 21 #9; ON 23 #4; ON 24 #14; ON 30 #2; ON 32 #25; ON 33 #20; ON 35 #15; ON 36 #6; ON 37 #6; ON 38 #10; ON 40 #7

CARMEN JONES (Bizet; arr. Bennett)   29, 41, 42

CARMINA BURANA (Orff)   13, 25, 69

CARNIVAL (Merrill)   29, 65

CARNIVAL FAIRY   see   FASCHINGSFEE

CAROUSEL (Rodgers, R.)   29, 41, 42, 65

CARRION CROW (Fletcher)   25

CARROSSE DU SAINT-SACRAMENT (Berners)   15, 18

CARRY NATION (Moore)   23, 25

CASINO GIRL (Englander)   29

CASTAWAY (Berkeley)   71

CASTLE AGRAZANT (Lyford)   73

CASTLES IN THE AIR (Kerker)   29

CASTOR AND POLLUX (Rameau)   25, 60, 64

CAT AND THE FIDDLE (Kern)   29, 41, 42

CATERINA CORNARO (Donizetti)   25

CATILINE CONSPIRACY (Hamilton)   MT 115 #1573 p.
210; MT 115 #1575 p. 411

CATULLI CARMINA (Orff)   25, 69

CAULDRON OF THE ANNWN   see   BRONWEN; CHILD-
REN OF DON; DYLAN, SON OF THE WAVE

CAVALIER OF THE ROSE   see   ROSENKAVALIER

CAVALLERIA RUSTICANA (Mascagni)   01, 02, 03, 04,
06, 07, 09, 11, 12, 14, 15, 18, 19, 20, 24, 27, 30,
31, 32, 33, 34, 35, 36, 39, 40, 42, 45, 46, 47, 48,
49, 50, 51, 56, 57, 58, 60, 61, 62, 64, 66, 67, 68,
69, 70, 74; ON 15 #19; ON 16 #12; ON 17 #22; ON 21
#22; ON 23 #9; ON 24 #13; ON 27 #5; ON 28 #22; ON
34 #15; ON 35 #16; ON 39 #11

CECILIA (Refice)   NY 1/10/77 p. 78

CELEBRATION (Schmidt)   29, 65

CELTIC TALE   see   IERNIN

CENA DELLE BEFFE (Giordano)   01, 60, 64, 66, 73

CENDRILLON (Massenet)   01, 25, 32, 33, 64, 66

CENERENTOLA (Rossini)   03, 14, 15, 18, 19, 24, 28,
32, 33, 35, 36, 37, 40, 48, 49, 60, 61, 62, 64, 67,
69, 74; ON 30 #2

CENT VIERGES (Lecocq)   41

ČERT A KAČA   see   DEVIL AND KATE

ČERTOVA STĚNA   see   DEVIL'S WALL

CHANSON DE FORTUNIO (Offenbach)   25

CHANTICLEER (Barab)   24

CHANTICLEER (Barthelson)   25

CHARLATAN

CHARLATAN (Sousa) 05, 42

CHEMINEAU (Leroux) 01, 64, 73

CHEREVICHKI (Chaikovski) 10

CHIEFTAIN (Sullivan) 41

CHILD AND THE SORCERESS see ENFANT ET LES SORTILEGES

CHILDHOOD MIRACLE (Rorem) 24

CHILDREN OF DON (Holbrooke) 15, 18, 56, 64

CHILDLESS WOMAN see FRAU OHNE SCHATTEN

CHIMES OF NORMANDY see CLOCHES DE CORNE-VILLES

CHIN-CHIN (Caryll) 29

CHINESE HONEYMOON (Kerker & Talbot) 22, 29, 42

CHINESE PRINCESS see TURANDOT

CHOCOLATE SOLDIER (Straus) 21, 28, 41, 42

CHRIS AND THE WONDERFUL LAMP (Sousa) 05

CHRISTOFORO COLOMBO (Franchetti, Alberto) 01, 42

CHRISTOPHE COLOMB (Milhaud) 40, 48, 64, 74

CHRISTOPHER COLUMBUS (Offenbach; arr. White and Thomas) MT 117 #1603 p. 755

CHRISTOPHER SLY (Argento) 25

CHU CHIN CHOW (Norton) 22, 41

CIBOULETTE (Hahn) 41

CONVITATO DI PIETRA (Gazzaniga)   MT 114 #1569 p. 1157

COPPELIA (Delibes)   01

COQ D'OR (Rimskii-Korsakov)   01, 03, 04, 07, 10, 11, 12, 13, 15, 18, 19, 24, 26, 32, 33, 35, 36, 39, 40, 42, 47, 48, 49, 51, 60, 61, 62, 64, 66, 67, 68, 69, 70, 72, 73, 74

CORNELIA FAROLI (Kubelik)   25

CORONATION OF POPPEA   see   INCORONAZIONE DI POPPEA

CORREGIDOR (Wolf)   01, 40, 48, 64, 69, 74

COSA RARA (Martín y Soler)   48

COSI FAN TUTTE (Mozart)   01, 02, 03, 04, 07, 08, 11, 12, 14, 15, 18, 19, 24, 28, 31, 32, 33, 35, 36, 37, 39, 40, 42, 45, 49, 50, 51, 57, 58, 60, 61, 62, 64, 66, 67, 69, 70, 73, 74; ON 16 #10; ON 17 #14; ON 18 #22; ON 20 #6; ON 26 #22; ON 29 #15; ON 36 #9; ON 40 #8

COSTANZA E FORTEZZA (Fux)   64

COUNT OF LUXEMBOURG (Lehár)   19, 21, 28, 41, 42

COUNT ORY   see   COMTE ORY

COUNTESS MARITZ   see   GRAEFIN MARIZA

COUNTRY DOCTOR   see   LANDARZT

COUNTRY GIRL (Monckton)   22, 41

COUNTRY PHILOSOPHER   see   FILOSOFO DI CAM-PAGNO

COUSIN FROM NOWHERE   see   VETTER AUS DINGSDA

COX AND BOX (Sullivan)   41, 42

CRADLE WILL ROCK (Blitzstein) 23, 29

CRICKET ON THE HEARTH (Goldmark) 01, 02, 32, 33, 40, 42, 66

CRIME AND PUNISHMENT (Petrovics) 25

CRIME AND PUNISHMENT (Sutermeister) see RAS-KOLNIKOFF

CRISPINO E LA COMARE (Ricci, L. & F.) 01, 28, 32, 33, 34, 42, 60, 64, 73

CRISS CROSS (Kern) 29

CRISTOFORO COLOMBO see CHRISTOPHER COLUMBO

CRITIC (Stanford) 73

CROCIATO (Meyerbeer) MT 113 #1547 p. 39

CROWN DIAMONDS (Auber) 28, 42, 64

CROWN PRINCE see ZAREWITSCH

CRUCIBLE (Ward) 13, 23, 25

CUBANA, OR A LIFE FOR ART (Henze) 25

CUNNING LITTLE VIXEN (Janáček) 25, 69, 74

CURLEW RIVER (Britten) 25, 74

CYRANO DE BERGERAC (Alfano) 73

CYRANO DE BERGERAC (Damrosch) 01, 32, 33, 42, 60, 64, 73

CZAAR UND ZIMMERMANN see ZAR UND ZIMMER-MANN

CZARDASFUERSTIN (Kálmán) 21, 41

CZAR'S BRIDE see TSAR'S BRIDE

-D-

DALIBOR (Smetana) 25, 40, 48, 64, 74

DAME BLANCHE (Boieldieu) 01, 02, 28, 34, 40, 42, 48, 60, 64, 69, 74

DAMES AT SEA (Wise) 29, 65

DAMN YANKEES (Adler, R. & Ross) 29, 41, 65

DAMNATION OF FAUST (Berlioz) 01, 04, 11, 13, 15, 17, 19, 25, 32, 33, 40, 42, 48, 61, 64, 68, 69, 74

DANCING MISTRESS (Monckton) 22

DANCING YEARS (Novello) 22, 28, 41

DANTE AND BEATRICE (Philpot) 15, 18

DANTONS TOD (Einem) 25, 69, 74

DAPHNE (Strauss, R.) 25, 40, 48, 69, 74

DARDANUS (Rameau) MT 114 #1562 p. 399

DARK WATERS (Křenek) 25

DAUGHTER OF MADAME ANGOT see FILLE DE MADAME ANGOT

DAUGHTER OF THE REGIMENT see FIGLIA DEL REGGIMENTO

DAY BEFORE SPRING (Loewe) 29

DEAD CITY see TOTE STADT

DEAD EYES see TOTEN AUGEN

DOCTOR AND THE APOTHECARY (Dittersdorf) 28

DOCTOR CUPID see AMORE MEDICO

DOCTOR FAUST see DOKTOR FAUST

DOCTOR IN SPITE OF HIMSELF see MEDECIN MAL-GRE LUI

DOCTOR JOHANNES FAUST (Reutter) 73

DOKTOR FAUST (Busoni) 25, 40, 69, 74

DOLLAR PRINCENSSIN (Fall) 21, 28, 41, 42

DOLLY VARDEN (Edwards) 42

DOLORES (Breton) 01, 66

DOMINO NOIR (Auber) 01, 02, 25, 28

DON CARLOS (Verdi) 01, 02, 03, 04, 06, 08, 11, 14, 15, 18, 19, 24, 32, 33, 35, 36, 37, 39, 40, 42, 45, 48, 49, 58, 60, 61, 62, 64, 67, 68, 69, 74; ON 16 #22; ON 17 #7; ON 19 #17; ON 23 #22; ON 25 #23; ON 28 #17; ON 30 #6; ON 34 #16

DON GIOVANNI (Mozart) 01, 02, 03, 04, 06, 07, 09, 11, 12, 14, 15, 18, 19, 20, 24, 26, 30, 31, 32, 33, 34, 35, 36, 37, 38, 39, 40, 42, 44, 45, 46, 47, 48, 49, 50, 52, 54, 56, 57, 58, 60, 61, 62, 63, 64, 66, 67, 68, 69, 70, 72, 74; ON 15 #11; ON 17 #5; ON 18 #18; ON 19 #14; ON 22 #6; ON 23 #15; ON 25 #10; ON 27 #11; ON 28 #7; ON 30 #13; ON 31 #14; ON 33 #10; ON 35 #21; ON 37 #17; ON 38 #23; ON 39 #13

DON JUAN (Mozart) see DON GIOVANNI

DON JUAN DE MAÑARA (Goossens) 15, 18, 64, 73

DON PASQUALE (Donizetti) 01, 02, 03, 04, 07, 11, 12, 14, 15, 18, 19, 24, 28, 32, 33, 34, 39, 40, 42, 45, 48, 49, 50, 51, 57, 58, 60, 61, 62, 64, 66, 67, 68, 69, 70, 74; ON 20 #14; ON 29 #9; ON 35 #6

DON PERLIMPLIN (Rieti) 24

DON QUICHOTTE (Massenet) 01, 04, 25, 40, 42, 48, 56, 64, 66, 73, 74

DON RODRIGO (Ginastera) 25

DONAUWEIBCHEN see LESTA, THE DNIEPIN WATER NYMPH

DONKEY'S SHADOW see ESELS SCHATTEN

DONNA DEL LAGO (Rossini) 74

DONNA DIANA (Reznicek) 02, 28

DONNA JUANITA (Suppé) 28, 42

DONNA SERPENTE (Casella) 73

DONNE CURIOSE (Wolf-Ferrari) 01, 25, 28, 32, 33, 42, 60, 64, 66, 68, 73

DON'T WE ALL? (Phillips, B.) 24

DOOR (Mopper) 24

DORF OHNE GLOCKE (Künneke) 41

DOROTHY (Cellier) 22, 41

DOUBLE TROUBLE (Mohaupt) 24

DOWN IN THE VALLEY (Weill) 24

DR. see DOCTOR

DRAGON OF WANTELY (Lampe) MT 113 #1547 p. 71

DRAGONS DE VILLARS (Maillart) 01, 02, 64

DREAM see REVE

DREAM OF LIN-TUNG see TRAUM DES LIU-TUNG

DREI PINTOS (Weber) 02, 64

DREI WALZER (Straus) 28, 41

DREIGROSCHENOPER see THREE PENNY OPERA

DREIMAEDERLHAUS (Schubert; arr. Berté) 21, 28, 41

DRESS (Bucci) 24

DUBARRY WAS A LADY (Porter) 29, 42

DUBROVSKY (Napravnik) 10

DUCHESS OF CHICAGO see HERZOGIN VON CHICAGO

DUCHESS OF DANTZIC (Caryll) 42

DUE FOSCARI (Verdi) 25, 74

DUEL BETWEEN TANCRED AND CLORINDA see COM-
BATTIMENTO DI TANCREDI E CLORINDA

DUENNA (Prokofiev) 24, 39, 74

DUKE BLUEBEARD'S CASTLE see BLUEBEARD'S
CASTLE

DUKE OR DEVIL (Gatty) 15, 18

DUMB GIRL OF PORTICI see MUETTE DE PORTICI

DUNSTAN AND THE DEVIL (Williamson) 25

DVE VDOVY (Smetana) 74

DYBBUK (Rocca) 73

DYBBUK (Tamkin) 23

DYEMON see DEMON

DYLAN, SON OF THE WAVE (Holbrooke) 15, 18

-E-

EARL AND THE GIRL (Caryll) 22, 42

EARL CARROLL'S VANITIES (Carroll) 29

ECLAIR (Halevy) 28, 42

EDUCATION MANQUEE (Chabrier) 24

EGYPTIAN HELEN (Strauss, R) 01, 15, 18, 25, 32, 33, 40, 42, 48, 64, 69, 73, 74

EGYPTIAN MARY see MARIA EGIZIACA

EIDIPO RE (Leoncavallo) 73

EIGHT SONGS FOR A MAD KING (Davies, P.) 25

EILEEN (Herbert) 41, 42

EINSTEIN (Wilson, R. & Glass) NY 12/13/76 p. 164

ELDA see LORELEY

ELECTRA (Strauss, R.) 01, 03, 04, 07, 11, 12, 14, 15, 18, 19, 24, 32, 33, 39, 40, 42, 46, 47, 48, 49, 50, 51, 56, 58, 60, 61, 62, 64, 66, 67, 69, 73, 74; ON 16 #16; ON 25 #20; ON 31 #7; ON 35 #18; ON 40 #10

ELEGY FOR YOUNG LOVERS (Henze) 25, 74

ELEPHANT STEPS (Silverman) 25

ELF KING'S OATH see OBERON

ELISABETTA, REGINA D'INGHILTERRA see ELIZA-BETH, QUEEN OF ENGLAND

ELISIR D'AMORE (Donizetti) 01, 03, 06, 11, 12, 14,
24, 27, 28, 32, 33, 34, 36, 37, 39, 40, 42, 45, 48,
49, 58, 60, 64, 66, 67, 68, 69, 73, 74; ON 14 #8; ON
25 #7; ON 30 #18; ON 32 #20; ON 36 #13; ON 38 #22

ELIXIR OF LOVE see ELISIR D'AMORE

ELIZABETH, QUEEN OF ENGLAND (Rossini) 15, 17, 74

EMEL'YAN PUGACHOV (Koval) 10

EMERALD ISLE (Sullivan) 22, 41

EMPEROR JONES (Gruenberg) 01, 04, 32, 33, 42, 48,
60, 64, 73

EMPRESS JOSEPHINE see KAISERIN JOSEPHINE

ENCHANTER (Holbrooke) 15, 18

ENDE EINER WELT (Henze) 25

ENFANT ET LES SORTILEGES (Ravel) 11, 15, 16, 19,
24, 48, 61, 67, 74

ENFANT PRODIGUE (Debussy) 01, 15, 18, 24, 42

ENLEVEMENT D'EUROPE see TROIS OPERAS-MIN-
UTES

ENTFUEHRUNG AUS DEM SERAIL see ABDUCTION
FROM THE SERAGLIO

EPHESIAN MATRON (Dibdin) MT 112 #1536 p. 156

EQUIVOCI (Storace) MT 115 #1574 p. 318

EQUIVOCI IN AMORE (Scarlatti, A.) MT 115 #1574 p. 32

ERISMENA (Cavalli) JAMS 28 #2 p. 283-4

ERMINIE (Jacobowski) 28, 34, 41, 42, 68

ERNANI (Verdi)   01, 03, 04, 13, 15, 18, 19, 25, 32,
33, 39, 40, 42, 48, 60, 61, 62, 64, 66, 67, 68, 74;
ON 21 #7; ON 27 #4; ON 29 #22

ERNEST IN LOVE (Prockriss)   65

ERO E LEANDRO (Mancinelli)   01, 64

ERO THE JOKER (Gotovac)   11

EROS VANQUEUR (Bréville)   73

ERWARTUNG (Schoenberg)   25, 74

ESCLARMONDE (Massenet)   66

ESCORIAL (Levy, M.)   24

ESELS SCHATTEN (Strauss, R.)   25

ESMERALDA (Thomas, Arthur)   64

ESTHER (Meyerowitz)   24

ESTHER DE CARPENTRAS (Milhaud)   73

ETOILE (Chabrier)   74

ETOILE DU NORD (Meyerbeer)   01, 15, 18; MT 116
#1584 p. 130-34

EUGENE ONEGIN (Chaikovskii)   01, 03, 04, 07, 10, 11,
12, 15, 18, 19, 24, 32, 33, 34, 35, 36, 39, 40, 42, 45,
48, 49, 50, 51, 60, 61, 62, 64, 66, 67, 68, 69, 70, 73,
74; ON 22 #5; ON 28 #16

EURIDICE (Peri)   69

EURYANTHE (Weber)   01, 02, 03, 04, 19, 25, 32, 33,
34, 40, 42, 48, 60, 64, 66, 69, 74

EVA (Lehár)   41

EVANGELIMANN (Kienzl)   01, 02, 32, 33, 42, 69

EVANGELINE (Rice)   29

EXCURSIONS OF MR. BROUCEK (Janáček)   25, 74

EZIO (Handel)   25

-F-

FABLE OF ORPHEUS   see   FAVOLA DI ORFEO

FABLES (Rorem)   25

FABRIKSMAEDEL   see   EVA

FACE THE MUSIC (Berlin)   29, 42

FADE OUT-FADE IN (Styne)   29

FAIR AT SOROCHINTZKY (Musorgskii)   10, 24, 32, 33,
40, 42, 48, 60, 64, 69, 73, 74

FAIR CO-ED (Luders)   29

FAIR MAID OF PERTH (Bizet)   15, 17, 19, 74

FAIRY QUEEN (Purcell, H.)   11, 19

FAIRYLAND (Parker)   01, 42, 56, 73

FALKA (Chassaigne)   34

FALLEN FAIRIES (German)   41

FALSTAFF (Verdi)   01, 02, 03, 04, 07, 08, 11, 12, 15,
16, 17, 19, 24, 31, 32, 33, 34, 35, 36, 37, 39, 40, 42,
47, 48, 49, 50, 51, 57, 58, 60, 61, 62, 64, 66, 67, 68,
69, 70, 73, 74; ON 28 #19; ON 29 #11; ON 32 #7; ON
36 #19; ON 39 #19

FAMILY AFFAIR (Kander) 65

FAMILY OF TARAS (Kabalevsky) 10

FANCIULLA DEL WEST (Puccini) 01, 03, 04, 13, 15,
18, 19, 24, 32, 33, 35, 36, 39, 40, 42, 48, 49, 56,
60, 61, 62, 64, 66, 67, 69, 70, 73, 74; ON 26 #8; ON
30 #10; ON 34 #20

FANNY (Rome) 29, 41, 65

FANTANA (Hubbell) 29

FANTASTICKS (Schmidt) 29, 65

FARSA AMOROSA (Zandonai) 73

FASCHINGSFEE (Kálmán) 41

FATAL WISHES see TOEDLICHEN WUENSHE

FATE (Janáček) MT 113 #1547 p. 34-35

FATINITZA (Suppé) 28, 41, 42

FAULE HANS see IDLE HANS

FAUN IN THE FOREST (Cockshott) 25

FAUST (Gounod) 01, 02, 03, 04, 06, 07, 09, 11, 12,
14, 15, 18, 19, 20, 24, 27, 30, 31, 32, 33, 34, 35,
36, 39, 40, 42, 43, 45, 46, 47, 48, 49, 55, 56, 57,
58, 60, 61, 62, 63, 64, 66, 67, 68. 69, 70, 74; ON 14
#9; ON 15 #9; ON 18 #4; ON 19 #15; ON 20 #13; ON
22 #9; ON 24 #7; ON 28 #8; ON 30 #23; ON 31 #9; ON
33 #12; ON 36 #14; ON 37 #8

FAVOLA DEL FIDIO CAMBIATO (Malipiero) 73

FAVOLA DI ORFEO (Casella) 24

FAVOLA D'ORFEO (Monteverdi) 03, 19, 24, 40, 48,
49, 60, 61, 62, 67, 69, 74

FAVORITA (Donizetti) 01, 04, 15, 17, 19, 32, 33, 34, 40, 42, 48, 60, 64, 68, 74

FAVOURITE see GUENSTLING

FEDORA (Giordano) 01, 04, 19, 32, 33, 34, 40, 42, 48, 60, 61, 64, 66, 73, 74

FEEN (Wagner, R.) 69

FELDLAGER IN SCHLESIEN (Meyerbeer) MT 116 #1584 p. 130-4

FEMME NEU (Février) 72

FÊTE CHEZ THERESE (Hahn) 01

FÊTE GALANTE (Smyth) 15, 18, 40, 42, 48

FÊTES D'HEBE (Rameau) MT 115 #1575 p. 404

FEUERSNOT (Strauss, R.) 15, 18, 32, 33, 34, 42, 60, 64, 66

FIAMMA (Respighi) 73

FIDDLER ON THE ROOF (Bock) 65

FIDELIO (Beethoven) 01, 02, 03, 04, 07, 08, 11, 12, 14, 15, 18, 19, 20, 24, 26, 31, 32, 33, 34, 35, 36, 37, 38, 39, 40, 42, 43, 44, 45, 47, 48, 49, 52, 54, 56, 57, 58, 60, 61, 62, 64, 66, 67, 68, 69, 70, 72, 74; ON 15 #20; ON 24 #15; ON 27 #12; ON 30 #12; ON 35 #10; ON 36 #16; ON 40 #13

FIERA (Cremesini) 73

FIERA DI SOROCINZI see FAIR AT SOROCHINTZKY

FIERRABRAS (Schubert) MT 112 #1538 p. 338-9

FIERY ANGEL see ANGE DE FEU

64, 66, 67, 68, 69, 70, 72, 73, 74; ON 15 #10; ON 24
#18; ON 27 #13; ON 29 #14; ON 32 #13; ON 34 #14

FLOOD (Stravinsky) 25

FLORIMEL, OR LOVE'S REVENGE (Greene) MT 114
#1569 p. 112-13

FLORODORA (Stuart) 22, 28, 34, 41, 42

FLOSS DER MEDUSA (Henze) MT 113 #1552 p. 588-9

FLOWER AND HAWK (Floyd) 25

FLOWER-DRUM SONG (Rodgers, R.) 22, 29, 41, 65

FLUT (Blacher) 24, 69

FLYING DUTCHMAN see FLIEGENDE HOELLANDER

FLYING HIGH (Henderson, R.) 29

FOLKUNGER (Kretschmer) 01, 02

FOLLOW THE GIRLS (Charig) 29

FOLLOW THRU (Henderson, R.) 29

FORCES OF DESTINY see FORZA DEL DESTINO

FOREST (Smyth) 15, 18

FORET BLEUE (Aubert) 73

FORTUNE TELLER (Herbert) 29, 41, 42

FORTY-FIVE MINUTES FROM BROADWAY (Cohan) 29,
41

FORZA DEL DESTINO (Verdi) 01, 03, 04, 06, 08, 11,
12, 14, 15, 17, 19, 24, 32, 33, 35, 36, 37, 39, 40, 42,
45, 47, 48, 49, 57, 58, 60, 61, 62, 64, 66, 67, 68,
69, 70, 73, 74; ON 17 #4; ON 18 #19; ON 20 #19; ON

22 #12; ON 24 #19; ON 26 #7; ON 29 #13; ON 32 #19; ON 36 #12; ON 39 #18

FOUR DAYS see QUATRE JOURNEES

FOUR NOTE OPERA (Johnson, T.) 25

FOUR RUFFIANS see QUATTRO RUSTEGHI

FOUR SAINTS IN THREE ACTS (Thomson) 04, 24, 39, 40, 48, 61, 62, 67, 74

FOX see RENARD

FRA DIAVOLO (Auber) 01, 02, 04, 15, 18, 19, 25, 28, 32, 33, 34, 40, 42, 48, 60, 64, 66, 68, 69, 74

FRA GHERARDO (Pizzetti) 60, 64, 73

FRANCESCA DA RIMINI (Rachmaninoff) 15, 18

FRANCESCA DA RIMINI (Zandonai) 01, 25, 32, 33, 40, 42, 48, 56, 60, 61, 64, 73, 74

FRANKLIN'S TALE (Sokoloff) 25

FRASQUITA (Lehár) 21, 28, 41

FRATE INNAMORATO (Pergolesi) 24

FRAU LUNA (Lincke) 21, 28, 41

FRAU OHNE KUSS (Kollo) 41

FRAU OHNE SCHATTEN (Strauss, R.) 11, 13, 19, 24, 40, 48, 49, 64, 67, 69, 73, 74; ON 31 #8; ON 33 #19; ON 35 #12

FRAUENLOB (Becker) 01

FREE LANCE (Sousa) 05

FREE-SHOOTER see FREISCHUETZ

FREISCHUETZ (Weber) 01, 02, 03, 04, 08, 11, 12,
14, 15, 18, 19, 24, 26, 32, 33, 34, 35, 36, 37, 39,
40, 42, 43, 48, 49, 52, 54, 56, 60, 61, 62, 64, 66,
67, 68, 69, 70, 72, 73, 74; ON 36 #21

FRIEDENSENGEL (Wagner, S.) MT 117 #1595 p. 53

FRIEDENSTAG (Strauss, R.) 25, 40, 48, 69, 74; MT
112 #1539 p. 439

FRIEDERIKE (Lehár) 21, 28, 41

FRIEND FRITZ see AMICO FRITZ

FROM DAY TO DAY see VON HEUTE AUF MORGEN

FROM THE HOUSE OF THE DEAD (Janáček) 25, 74

FROM THE SECOND CITY (Mathieu) 29

FUNNY FACE (Gershwin) 29

FUNNY GIRL (Styne) 29, 65

FUNNY THING HAPPENED ON THE WAY TO THE FOR-
UM (Sondheim) 29, 65

-G-

GALE (Leginska) 73

GALLANTRY (Moore) 24

GAMBLER (Prokofiev) 25, 74

GAME OF CHANCE (Barab) 24

GAME OF LOVE AND CHANCE see JEU DE L'AMOUR
ET DU HASARD

GARDEN OF ARTEMIS, OR APOLLO'S REVELS (Pinkham) 25

GIFT OF THE MAGI (Magney) 25

GINGHAM GIRL (Tilzer) 29

GIOCONDA (Ponchielli) 01, 03, 04, 08, 12, 14, 15,
18, 19, 24, 32, 33, 34, 39, 40, 42, 46, 47, 48, 56,
57, 58, 60, 61, 62, 64, 66, 67, 68, 74; ON 17 #9; ON
19 #21; ON 21 #23; ON 23 #10; ON 25 #21; ON 26 #20;
ON 31 #25; ON 32 #18; ON 40 #20

GIOIELLI DELLA MADONA see JEWELS OF THE
MADONNA

GIORNO DI REGNO (Verdi) 74

GIOVANNA D'ARCO (Verdi) 13

GIOVANNI GALLURESE (Montemezzi) 60, 64

GIRL CRAZY (Gershwin) 22, 29, 41

GIRL FRIEND (Rodgers, R.) 22, 29

GIRL FROM UTAH (Rubens) 29

GIRL IN PINK TIGHTS (Romberg) 29

GIRL IN THE TAXI see KEUSCHE SUZANNE

GIRL OF THE GOLDEN WEST see FANCIULLA DEL
WEST

GIROFLE-GIROFLA (Lecocq) 28, 34, 41, 42

GIRONDINS (Le Borne) 01

GISMONDA (Février) 42, 73

GIUDITTA (Lehár) 21, 41

GIULIO CESARE (Handel) 03, 13, 24, 60, 61, 62, 64,
67, 69, 74

GIULIO CESARE (Malipiero) 73

GIURAMENTO (Mercandante) 25

GLAMOROUS NIGHT (Novello) 22, 41

GLASS BLOWERS see AMERICAN MAID

GLITTERING GATE (Glanville-Hicks) 25

GLORIANA (Britten) 11, 15, 25, 28, 40, 48, 71, 74

GLUECKLICHE HAND (Schoenberg) 69, 73

GLUECKLICHE REISE (Künneke) 41

GOETTERDAEMMERUNG (Wagner, R.) 01, 03, 04, 11, 12, 14, 15, 18, 19, 20, 24, 26, 30, 31, 32, 33, 34, 35, 36, 37, 39, 40, 42, 43, 45, 47, 48, 49, 52, 53, 56, 57, 58, 60, 61, 62, 64, 66, 67, 68, 69, 72, 74; ON 15 #17; ON 16 #9; ON 21 #16; ON 26 #11; ON 28 #5; ON 38 #20; ON 39 #15

GOING UP (Hirsch) 29

GOLDEN APPLE (Moross) 29, 65

GOLDEN BOY (Strouse) 29, 65

GOLDEN COCKEREL see COQ D'OR

GOLDEN CROSS (Brüll) 02, 34, 42

GOLDEN LION (Kechley) 25

GOLDEN RAINBOW (Marks) 29

GOLDENE MEISTERIN (Eysler) 41

GOLDILOCKS (Anderson) 65

GOLDSCHMIED VON TOLEDO (Offenbach) 15, 1º

GREAT WALTZ (Strauss, J.) 29

GREEK PASSION see GRIECHISCHE PASSION

GREEK SLAVE (Jones, Sidney) 22

GREYSTEEL (Gatty) 15, 18

GRIECHISCHE PASSION (Martinu) 25

GRISELDIS (Massenet) 01, 32, 33, 56, 66, 73

GROWING CASTLE (Williamson) 25

GUARANY (Gomez) 68

GUENSTLING (Wagner-Régeny) 69, 73

GUILLAUME TELL see WILLIAM TELL

GUNTRAM (Strauss, R.) 32, 33, 64

GUSTAV III (Auber) 01, 02

GUYS AND DOLLS (Loesser) 29, 41, 42, 48, 65

GWENDOLINE (Chabrier) 01, 64

GYPSY (Styne) 29, 41, 65

GYPSY BARON see ZIGEUNERBARON

GYPSY LOVE (Lehár) 21, 28, 41, 42

GYPSY PRINCESS see CZARDASFUERSTIN

-H-

H. M. S. PINAFORE see PINAFORE

HABANERA (Laparra) 01, 64, 73

HADDON HALL (Sullivan) 41

HAIR (MacDermot) 29, 65

HAIRCUT (Morgenstern) 25

HALF A SIXPENCE (Heneker) 65

HALKA (Moniuszko) 60

HALLELUJAH, BABY! (Styne) 29

HAMLET (Szokolay) 25

HAMLET (Thomas, Ambroise) 01, 02, 04, 19, 25,
42, 60, 64, 66, 68

HAND OF BRIDGE (Barber) 25

HANGING JUDGE (Lockwood) 25

HANS HEILING (Marschner) 02, 25, 32, 33, 34, 60, 64, 66

HAN'S KINGDOM see HONZOVA KRALOVSTVI

HANSEL AND GRETEL (Humperdinck) 01, 02, 03, 04,
07, 08, 11, 12, 14, 15, 18, 19, 20, 24, 26, 28, 32,
33, 34, 35, 36, 39, 40, 42, 43, 46, 47, 48, 55, 60,
61, 62, 64, 66, 67, 68, 69, 70, 72, 73, 74; ON 32 #8;
ON 36 #6; ON 40 #8

HAPPY HUNTING (Karr) 29, 65

HAPPY PRINCE (Williamson) 25

HAPPY TIME (Kander) 29

HARLEQUIN see ARLECCHINO

HARLEQUINADE PANTOMINES (Cole) MT 113 #1547
p. 38

HARY JANOS (Kodály) 40, 48, 74

HERZOGIN VON CHICAGO (Kálmán)   41

HEURE ESPAGNOLE (Ravel)   01, 03, 04, 07, 11, 15,
18, 19, 24, 28, 32, 33, 40, 42, 48, 49, 51, 60, 61,
62, 64, 66, 67, 69, 73, 74

HIGH BUTTON SHOES (Styne)   29

HIGH JINKS (Friml)   29

HIGH SPIRITS (Martin, H. & Gray)   29

HIGHWAYMAN (Koven)   29, 42

HIN UND ZURUECK (Hindemith)   24

HISTOIRE DU SOLDAT (Stravinsky)   15, 17, 24, 69, 74

HIT THE DECK (Youmans)   22, 29, 41

HOCHZEITSMORGEN (Kaskel)   02

HOHEIT TANZT WALZER (Ascher)   41

HOLD EVERYTHING (Henderson, R.)   29

HOLD ON TO YOUR HATS (Lane)   29

HOLLANDWEIBCHEN (Kálmán)   41

HOLY MOUNTAIN see HEILIGE BERG

HONEYDEW (Zimbalist)   29

HONEYMOON LANE (Hanley)   29

HONZOVA KRALOVSTVI (Ostreil)   73

HOORAY FOR WHAT? (Arlen)   29

HORSPFAL (Stokes)   25

HOUSE OF FLOWERS (Arlen)   29

INVISIBLE CITY OF KITEZH see KITEZH

IOLANTA (Chaikovskii) 10, 15, 18, 25, 74

IOLANTHE (Sullivan) 04, 19, 28, 34, 41, 42, 66

IPHIGENIA IN AULIS (Gluck) 01, 02, 07, 15, 17, 19,
24, 32, 33, 34, 40, 42, 48, 64, 73, 74

IPHIGENIA IN TARIS (Gluck) 01, 02, 07, 15, 17, 24,
32, 33, 34, 40, 42, 48, 60, 64, 69, 73, 74

IRENE (Tierney) 22, 29

IRIS (Mascagni) 01, 15, 18, 25, 32, 33, 40, 42, 48,
60, 64, 66, 68, 73, 74

IRISCHE LEGENDE (Egk) 69

IRMA LA DOUCE (Monnot) 41, 65

IRMELIN (Delius) 19, 25; ON 27 #8 p. 33

IRRLICHT (Grammann) 02

ISABEAU (Mascagni) 01, 73

ISLAND GOD (Menotti) 32, 33, 42

ISLAND OF TULIPATAN see ILE DE TULIPATAN

ISLE OF CHAMPAGNE (Furst) 29, 42

IT HAPPENED IN NORDLAND (Herbert) 29, 42

ITALIANA IN ALGERI (Rossini) 15, 17, 19, 24, 28, 29,
32, 33, 40, 48, 60, 61, 64, 69, 74; ON 38 #6; ON 39
#9

IT'S A BIRD, IT'S A PLANE, IT'S SUPERMAN (Strouse)
29, 65

IVAN SUSANIN see LIFE FOR THE TSAR

IVAN THE TERRIBLE see PSKOVITYANKA

IVANHOE (Sullivan) 64

IVROGNE CORRIGE (Gluck) 25

-J-

JACK AND THE BEANSTALK (Gruenberg) 73

JACOBIN (Dvorak) 25

JAMAICA (Arlen) 29

JEALOUS HUSBAND see GELOSO SCHERNITO

JEAN DE PARIS (Boieldieu) 01, 02

JEANNE D'ARC AU BUCHER (Honegger) 15, 16, 25, 69

JENNY'S WEDDING see NOCES DE JEANNETTE

JENUFA (Janáček) 13, 15, 16, 25, 40, 48, 49, 60, 64, 67, 69, 73, 74; ON 39 #8

JEREMIAH (Fink) 25

JESSONDA (Spohr) 01, 02

JEU DE L'AMOUR ET DU HASARD (Petit) 24

JEWELS OF THE MADONNA (Wolf-Ferrari) 01, 15, 18, 25, 32, 33, 39, 40, 42, 48, 56, 60, 64, 66, 68, 73, 74

JEWESS see JUIVE

JILL DARLING (Ellis) 22

JOAN OF ARC AT THE STAKE see JEANNE D'ARC AU BUCHER

JOHN SOCMAN (Lloyd)   15, 16

JOHNNY JOHNSON (Weill)   29, 41

JOHNNY PLAYS ON   see   JONNY SPIELT AUF

JOLIE FILLE DE PERTH   see   FAIR MAID OF PERTH

JOLLY ROGER, OR THE ADMIRAL'S DAUGHTER (Leigh)
41

JONGLEUR DE NOTRE DAME (Massenet)   01, 04, 07,
15, 18, 25, 32, 33, 34, 40, 42, 48, 60, 64, 66, 68,
73, 74

JONNY SPIELT AUF (Křenek)   01, 32, 33, 42, 60, 64,
69

JOSEPH (Méhul)   01, 02, 60, 64

JOTA (Laparra)   01

JOY (Brown)   29

JOYOUS SOUL   see   ANIMA ALLEGRA

JUBILEE (Porter)   29, 42

JUDGMENT OF PARIS (Purcell, D.)   MT 113 #1557 p.
1078

JUDGMENT OF ST. FRANCIS (Flagello)   25

JUDITH (Goossens)   15, 18, 73

JUDITH (Honegger)   64, 66, 73

JUGGLER OF NOTRE DAME   see   JONGLEUR DE
NOTRE DAME

JUGGLER OF OUR LADY (Kay)   25

JUIVE (Halevy) 01, 02, 03, 04, 12, 13, 15, 18, 19, 25, 32, 33, 34, 40, 42, 48, 51, 60, 64, 66, 73, 74

JULIEN (Charpentier) 73

JULIUS CAESAR see GIULIO CESARE

JULIUS CAESAR JONES (Williamson) 25

JUMBO (Rodgers, R.) 29

JUMPING FROG OF CALAVERAS COUNTY (Foss) 24

JUNGE LORD (Henze) 25, 74

JUNKER HEINZ (Perfall) 02

-K-

KAISERIN JOSEPHINE (Kálmán) 41

KARNEVAL IN ROM (Strauss, J.) 41

KASHCHEY THE IMMORTAL (Rimskii-Korsakov) 10

KAT'A KABANOVA (Janáček) 11, 15, 16, 25, 35, 36, 40, 48, 49, 69, 74

KATERINA ISMAILOVA (Shostakovich) 25, 74

KATINKA (Friml) 42

KATJA, DIE TAENZERIN (Gilbert, J.) 41

KEKSZAKALLU HERCEG VARA see BLUEBEARD'S CASTLE

KEUSCHE SUZANNE (Gilbert, J.) 41

KHOVANSHCHINA (Musorgskii) 04, 10, 13, 15, 18, 19, 25, 32, 33, 40, 42, 48, 49, 60, 64, 69, 73, 74; ON 14 #17

KID BOOTS (Tierney) 29

KING AGAINST HIS WILL (Chabrier) 01, 02, 19, 28, 74

KING ALFRED AND THE CAKES (Gatty) 15, 18

KING AND I (Rodgers, R.) 22, 29, 41, 65

KING ARTHUR (Purcell, H.) 71

KING CAROTTE see ROI CAROTTE

KING DODO (Luders) 29, 42

KING OEDIPUS (Leoncavallo) see EIDIPO RE

KING OEDIPUS (Stravinsky) see OEDIPUS REX

KING OF LAHORE (Massenet) 15, 18, 64, 66, 68

KING OF THE STUDENTS see BASOCHE

KING OF YS see ROI D'YS

KING PRIAM (Tippett) 25, 74

KING ROGER (Szymanowski) 74; MT 116 #1587 p. 435

KING SAID SO see ROI L'A DIT

KING THEODORE IN VENICE see RE TEODORO IN VENEZIA

KING'S BREAKFAST (Barthelson) 25

KING'S CHILDREN see KOENIGSKINDER

KING'S HENCHMAN (Taylor) 01, 04, 32, 33, 42, 60, 64, 66, 73

KING'S RHAPSODY (Novello) 22, 28, 41

-L-

LADIES FIRST (Sloane) 29

LADIES' VOICES (Martin V.) 25

LADY BE GOOD (Gershwin) 22, 29, 41

LADY IN ERMINE (Gilbert, J. & Goodman) 29

LADY IN LOTTERY see DEMOISELLE EN LOTERIE

LADY IN THE DARK (Weill) 29, 41

LADY MACBETH OF MTSENSK (Shostakovich) 01, 39, 60, 64, 69, 73

LADY MADCAP (Rubens) 28

LADY MOLLY see MY LADY MOLLY

LAFFING ROOM ONLY (Lane) 29

LAKME (Delibes) 01, 03, 04, 08, 12, 14, 15, 18, 19, 24, 32, 33, 34, 39, 40, 42, 47, 48, 51, 60, 61, 62, 64, 66, 67, 68, 74

LAND OF SMILES (Lehár) 19, 21, 28, 41

LANDARZT (Henze) 25

LANDESTREICHER (Ziehrer) 28

LANGE WEIHNACHTSMAHL (Hindemith) 25

LANGWIERIGE WEG IN DIE WOHNUNG DER NATASCHA UNGEHEUER (Henze) 25

LANZELOT (Dessau) MT 112 #1541 p. 685-6

LAST OF THE MOHICANS (Henderson, A.) NY 7/3/76 p. 69-71

LITTLE DUTCH GIRL see HOLLANDWEIBCHEN

LITTLE HARLEQUINADE (Salieri) 24

LITTLE JESSIE JAMES (Archer) 29

LITTLE JOHNNY JONES (Cohan) 29, 41

LITTLE MARY SUNSHINE (Besoyan) 29, 65

LITTLE ME (Coleman) 29

LITTLE MICHUS see P'TITES MICHU

LITTLE MILLIONAIRE (Cohan) 29

LITTLE SWEEP see LET'S MAKE AN OPERA

LITTLE TYCOON (Spencer) 29, 42

LIZZIE BORDEN (Kenward) 23, 25

LOAFER AND THE LOAF (Clarke) 24

LOBETANZ (Thuille) 01, 32, 33, 42

LODOLETTA (Mascagni) 01, 19, 32, 33, 42, 60, 64, 73

LOHENGRIN (Wagner, R.) 01, 02, 03, 04, 06, 07, 09, 11, 12, 14, 15, 18, 19, 20, 24, 26, 30, 31, 32, 33, 34, 35, 36, 37, 39, 40, 42, 43, 45, 47, 48, 49, 53, 56, 57, 58, 60, 61, 62, 63, 64, 66, 67, 68, 69, 70, 72, 74; ON 14 #10; ON 17 #23; ON 20 #7; ON 23 #13; ON 28 #12; ON 31 #13; ON 32 #5

LOMBARDS (Verdi) 15, 17, 25, 64, 68, 74

LONG CHRISTMAS DINNER see LANGE WEIHNACHTS-MAHL

LORD ARTHUR SAVILE'S CRIME (Bush, G.) MT 114 #1560 p. 169

LORD BYRON (Thomson)   MT 113 #1553 p. 689; NY 1/17/77 p. 106

LORD BYRON'S LOVE LETTER (Banfield) 24

LORELEY (Catalani) 01, 19, 42, 60, 66

LORLE (Förster) 02

LOST IN THE STARS (Weill) 23, 29, 41, 42

LOST SHEEP see BREBIS EGAREE

LOUISE (Charpentier) 01, 03, 04, 08, 11, 12, 14, 15, 18, 19, 24, 27, 32, 33, 34, 39, 40, 42, 47, 48, 51, 60, 61, 62, 64, 66, 67, 68, 69, 70, 73, 74

LOUISIANA PURCHASE (Berlin) 29

LOVE ADRIFT see LIEBE IM SCHNEE

LOVE FOR THREE ORANGES (Prokofiev) 03, 04, 14, 15, 16, 19, 24, 32, 33, 39, 40, 42, 48, 60, 61, 64, 67, 73, 74

LOVE LIFE (Weill) 29

LOVE OF DANAE see LIEBE DER DANAE

LOVE OF THE THREE KINGS see AMORE DEI TRE RE

LOVELY LADY (Stamper & Levy, H.) 29

LOVERS' FESTIVAL see FÊTE GALANTE

LOVE'S AWAKENING see WENN LIEBE ERWACHT

LOVE'S BATTLE (Meyer-Helmund) 01, 02

LOWLAND SEA (Wilder) 24

LOWLANDS see TIEFLAND

LUCEDIA (Giannini) 73

LUCIA DI LAMMERMOOR (Donizetti) 01, 02, 03, 04,
06, 09, 12, 14, 15, 18, 19, 20, 24, 27, 30, 31, 32,
33, 34, 35, 36, 37, 39, 40, 42, 45, 47, 48, 49, 56,
57, 58, 60, 61, 62, 64, 66, 67, 68, 69, 70, 74; ON
14 #11; ON 16 #8; ON 18 #12; ON 20 #10; ON 21 #4;
ON 22 #22; ON 26 #4; ON 29 #4; ON 30 #16; ON 31
#10; ON 33 #14; ON 37 #24

LUCIO SILLA (Mozart) 25

LUCKY DOLLAR (Kanitz) 25

LUCKY HAND see GLUECKLICHE HAND

LUCREZIA (Respighi) 73

LUCREZIA BORGIA (Donizetti) 01, 02, 04, 15, 18, 25,
27, 32, 33, 34, 40, 42, 48, 60, 64, 66, 67, 68, 74

LUISA MILLER (Verdi) 01, 13, 15, 17, 19, 25, 40, 42,
48, 60, 61, 64, 67, 73, 74; ON 32 #16; ON 36 #4

LULU (Berg) 13, 25, 40, 48, 49, 67, 69, 73, 74

LURLINE (Wallace) 15, 18, 34

LUSTIGE KRIEG see MERRY WAR

LUSTIGE WITWE see MERRY WIDOW

LUSTIGEN WEIBER VON WINDSOR see MERRY WIVES
OF WINDSOR

-M-

MA MIE ROSETTE (Lacome & Caryll) 41

MACBETH (Verdi) 03, 04, 11, 13, 19, 24, 33, 39, 40,
45, 48, 49, 60, 64, 67, 68, 69, 74; ON 23 #16; ON 24
#9; ON 26 #19; ON 28 #21; ON 37 #13

MACCABEES (Rubinstein)   01, 02

MADAM ANGOT'S DAUGHTER   see   FILLE DE MADAME
ANGOT

MADAME BUTTERFLY (Puccini)   01, 03, 04, 06, 07,
09, 11, 12, 14, 15, 18, 19, 24, 27, 30, 31, 32, 33, 34,
35, 36, 39, 40, 42, 45, 46, 47, 48, 49, 50, 52, 55, 56,
57, 58, 60, 61, 62, 64, 66, 67, 68, 69, 70, 73, 74;
ON 14 #16; ON 16 #13; ON 17 #11; ON 21 #5; ON 22
#21; ON 23 #8; ON 24 #24; ON 26 #12; ON 29 #20; ON
30 #2 and #9; ON 31 #21; ON 32 #22; ON 34 #19; ON
35 #25; ON 38 #21; ON 39 #10; ON 40 #19

MADAME CHRYSANTHEME (Messager)   01, 42

MADAME IMPERIA (Alfano)   73

MADAME POMPADOUR (Fall)   21, 28, 41

MADAME SANS-GENE (Giordano)   01, 32, 33, 42, 56,
60, 64, 66, 73

MADAME SHERRY (Hoschna)   29, 41, 42

MADELEINE (Herbert)   01, 32, 33, 42, 60, 64, 68, 73

MADEMOISELLE FIFI (Cui)   15, 18

MADEMOISELLE MODESTE (Herbert)   29, 41, 42

MAESTRO DI MUSICA (Pergolesi)   19, 24, 61, 73

MAGGIE FLYNN (Peretti)   65

MAGIC FIDDLE   see   ZAUBERGEIGE

MAGIC FLUTE (Mozart)   01, 02, 03, 04, 07, 09, 11,
12, 14, 15, 18, 19, 24, 26, 28, 30, 31, 32, 33, 34, 35,
36, 37, 39, 40, 42, 45, 46, 47, 48, 49, 50, 52, 54, 57,
58, 60, 61, 62, 64, 66, 67, 68, 69, 70, 72, 73, 74;
ON 20 #17; ON 21 #17; ON 23 #5; ON 28 #11; ON 31
#19; ON 32 #10; ON 34 #12; ON 37 #8; ON 38 #7

MAGIC FOUNTAIN (Delius) ON 27 #8 p. 33

MAGIC VIOLIN see ZAUBERGEIGE

MAGIC WINE see VIN HERBE

MAHAGONNY see RISE AND FALL OF THE CITY
MAHAGONNY

MAID MARIAN (Koven) 42

MAID OF ARLES see ARLESIANA

MAID OF ORLEANS (Chaikovskii) 74

MAID OF PSKOV see PSKOVITYANKA

MAID OF THE MOUNTAINS (Fraser-Simson) 22, 41

MAIDENS OF SCHILDA (Förster) 01, 02

MAIDS OF JAPAN see MOUSME

MAISKAYA NOCH see MAY NIGHT

MAKROPOULOS AFFAIR (Janáček) 25, 74

MALADY OF LOVE (Engel) 24

MALHEURS D'ORPHEE (Milhaud) 24

MAME (Herman) 29, 65

MAMELLES DE TIRESIAS (Poulenc) 24, 45, 71, 74

MAM'ZELLE FIFI see MADEMOISELLE FIFI

MAM'ZELLE NITOUCHE (Hervé) 21, 28, 41

MAN IN THE MOON see MONDO DELLA LUNA

MAN OF LA MANCHA (Leigh) 29, 65

MAN ON THE BEARSKIN RUG (Ramsier) 25

MAN WITHOUT A COUNTRY (Damrosch) 32, 33, 42, 60, 64, 73

MANON (Massenet) 01, 03, 04, 07, 09, 12, 14, 19, 24, 27, 30, 32, 33, 34, 35, 36, 39, 40, 42, 45, 46, 47, 48, 49, 50, 56, 57, 58, 60, 61, 64, 66, 67, 68, 69, 70, 74; ON 16 #6; ON 19 #6; ON 24 #6; ON 28 #6

MANON LESCAUT (Puccini) 01, 03, 04, 06, 08, 11, 12, 14, 15, 18, 19, 24, 32, 33, 34, 40, 42, 45, 48, 49, 58, 60, 61, 62, 64, 66, 67, 68, 69, 70, 73, 74; ON 14 #6; ON 20 #21; ON 23 #11; ON 25 #5; ON 30 #19; ON 32 #21; ON 38 #9; ON 39 #17

MANRU (Paderewski) 01, 32, 33, 34, 64, 73

MANY MOONS (Dougherty) 25

MARCHAND DE VENISE (Hahn) 73

MARGA (Pittrich) 01, 02

MARI A LA PORTE (Offenbach) 25, 41

MARIA EGIZIACA (Respighi) 73

MARIA GOLOVIN (Menotti) 23, 24

MARIA MALIBRAN (Bennett) 73

MARIA PADILLA (Donizetti) MT 114 #1564 p. 619-20

MARIA STUARDA (Donizetti) 13, 25, 74

MARIAGE AUX LANTERNES (Offenbach) 25, 41

MARIANA (Arrieta) 25

MARITANA (Wallace) 01, 15, 18, 28, 34, 40, 42, 66, 68, 74

MARKHEIM (Floyd) 25

MÂROUF, LE SAVETIER DU CAIRE (Rabaud) 01, 28, 32, 33, 40, 42, 48, 60, 64, 73, 74

MARRIAGE (Martinu) 24

MARRIAGE (Musorgskii) 10

MARRIAGE BY LANTERNLIGHT see MARIAGE AUX LANTERNES

MARRIAGE CONTRACT see CAMBIALE DI MATRIMO- NIO

MARRIAGE OF FIGARO see NOZZI DI FIGARO

MARRIAGE OF JEANNETTE see NOCES DE JEAN- NETTE

MARRIAGE OF OLIVETTE see NOCES D'OLIVETTE

MARTHA (Flotow) 01, 02, 04, 12, 14, 15, 18, 19, 24, 26, 28, 32, 33, 34, 39, 40, 42, 43, 47, 56, 60, 61, 62, 64, 66, 67, 68, 69, 72, 74; ON 25 #16; ON 32 #14

MARTYRE DE SAINT SEBASTIAN (Debussy) 66

MARTYRED (Wade) 25

MARY (Hirsch) 29

MASANIELLO see MUETTE DE PORTICI

MASANIELLO FURIOSO (Keiser) MT 114 #1569 p. 1105-6

MASCOTTE (Audran) 21, 28, 34, 41, 42

MASKARADE (Nielsen) 25, 74

MASKED BALL see BALLO IN MASCHERA

MASON (Auber) 01, 02

MASQUE OF ANGELS (Argento) 25

MASQUERADE see MASKARADE

MASSADA 967 (Tal)   MT 114 #1568 p. 1043

MASSIMILLA DONI (Schoeck)   73

MASTER PETER'S PUPPET SHOW see RETABLO DE
MAESE PEDRO

MASTER THIEF (Lindner) 02

MASTERSINGERS OF NUREMBERG see MEISTERSING-
ER VON NUERNBERG

MATHIS DER MALER (Hindemith) 11, 15, 16, 19, 24,
40, 42, 48, 69, 74

MATRIMONIO SEGRETO (Cimarosa) 15, 17, 19, 24, 28,
32, 33, 34, 39, 40, 42, 48, 60, 61, 62, 64, 69, 73, 74

MAURER see MASON

MAVRA (Stravinsky) 15, 18, 24, 28, 60, 64, 69, 73, 74

MAXIMILIEN (Milhaud) 73

MAY NIGHT (Rimskii-Korsakov) 10, 15, 18, 25, 42, 74

MAY WINE (Romberg) 29

MAYTIME (Romberg) 29, 41, 42

MAZEPPA (Chaikovskii) 10, 74

ME AND JULIET (Rodgers, R.) 29, 65

ME AND MY GIRL (Gay) 22

MEADOW OF THE SCHOLARS see PRE AUX CLERCS

MEDECIN MALGRE LUI (Gounod) 24, 28

MEDEE   77

MEDEE (Cherubini)   24, 60, 64, 67, 69, 74

MEDEE (Milhaud)   24

MEDICI (Leoncavallo)   34

MEDICO E LA MORTE   see   CRISPENO E LA COMARE

MEDIUM (Menotti)   11, 14, 15, 16, 23, 24, 32, 33, 39,
40, 42, 45, 46, 48, 61, 62, 67, 74

MEFISTOFELE (Boito)   01, 03, 12, 14, 15, 18, 19, 25,
32, 33, 34, 39, 40, 42, 48, 60, 61, 62, 64, 66, 67, 68, 74

MEINE SCHWESTER UND ICH (Benatzky)   28

MEISTERSINGER VON NUERNBERG (Wagner, R.)   01,
02, 03, 04, 07, 09, 11, 12, 14, 15, 18, 19, 20, 24, 26,
30, 31, 32, 33, 34, 35, 36, 37, 39, 40, 42, 44, 45, 46,
47, 48, 49, 53, 56, 57, 58, 60, 61, 62, 64, 66, 67, 68,
69, 70, 72, 74; ON 16 #20; ON 17 #10; ON 19 #5; ON
20 #12; ON 23 #18; ON 27 #9; ON 31 #12; ON 33 #9;
ON 36 #8; ON 40 #21

MELUSINE (Grammann)   01, 02

MELUSINE (Reimann)   25; MT 112 #1544 p. 989

MEPHISTOPHELES   see   MEFISTOFELE

MEPRISES PAR RESSEMBLANCES (Grêtry)   MT 115
#1573 p. 243

MERCHANT OF VENICE   see   MARCHAND DE VENISE

MERLIN (Goldmark)   01, 02

MERMAID IN LOCK 7 (Siegmeister)   25

MERRIE ENGLAND (German)   19, 22, 28, 41

MERRY MOUNT (Hanson)   32, 33, 42, 60, 64, 73

MIREILLE (Gounod)   01, 15, 18, 19, 25, 32, 33, 40, 48, 60, 61, 64, 68, 74

MIRETTE (Messager)   41

MIRJANA (Mandic)   73

MISERLY KNIGHT (Rachmaninoff)   01, 10

MISS HELYETT (Audran)   41

MISS HOOK OF HOLLAND (Rubens)   22, 41

MISS JULIE (Rorem)   23, 25

MISS LIBERTY (Berlin)   29, 42

MISTAKEN IDENTITIES see MEPRISES PAR RESSEM-
BLANCES

MR. AND MRS. DISCOBBOLOS (Westergaard)   25

MR. BRUSCHINO see SIGNOR BRUSCHINO

MR. CINDERS (Ellis & Myers)   22

MISTER PRESIDENT (Berlin)   29, 65

MR. WIX OF WICKHAM (Darnley)   29

MISTER WONDERFUL (Bock)   29

MISTER WU (Albert)   73

MISTRESS MAID see SERVA PADRONA

MITRIDATE (Mozart)   MT 113 #1547 p. 41

MITRIDATE EUPATORE (Scarlatti, A.)   64

MLLE. MODISTE see MADEMOISELLE MODISTE

MODANNA IMPERIA see MADAME IMPERIA

MOZART

MOZART AND SALIERI (Rimskii-Korsakov) 10, 15, 18, 19

MR. see MISTER

MUCH ADO ABOUT NOTHING (Stanford) 73

MUETTE DE PORTICI (Auber) 01, 02, 15, 17, 25, 28, 32, 33, 34, 40, 48, 60, 64, 66, 69, 74

MULATTO see BARRIER

MULLIGAN GUARD'S BALL (Braham) 29

MURDER IN THE CATHEDRAL see ASSASSINIO NELLA CATTEDRALE

MUSIC FIRST, THEN THE WORD see PRIMA LA MUSICA, POI LE PAROLE

MUSIC IN THE AIR (Kern) 29, 41, 42

MUSIC MAN (Willson) 29, 41, 65

MUSIC MASTER see MAESTRO DI MUSICA

MY FAIR LADY (Loewe) 22, 29, 41, 65

MY HEART'S IN HIGHLAND (Beeson) 25

MY LADY MOLLY (Jones, Sidney) 22

MY MARYLAND (Romberg) 42

MY SISTER AND I see MEINE SCHWESTER UND ICH

MYSTERIUM (Scriabin) ON 31 #19 p. 6

MYSTICAL MISS see CHARLATAN

-N-

NABOTH'S VINEYARD (Goehr) 25

NABUCCO (Verdi) 11, 13, 15, 17, 19, 25, 40, 45, 48, 64, 67, 74; ON 25 #4

NACHT IN VENEDIG (Strauss, J.) 19, 21, 28, 41, 74

NACHTLAGER VON GRANADA (Kreutzer) 02, 34

NAMIKO-SAN (Franchetti, Aldo) 73

NANON (Genée) 34, 42

NATALIA PETROVNA (Hoiby) 23, 25

NATOMA (Herbert) 01, 32, 33, 42, 60, 64, 68, 73

NAUFRAGEURS see WRECKERS

NAUGHTY MARIETTA (Herbert) 22, 29, 41, 42

NAUSICAA (Glanville-Hicks) 25

NAUTCH GIRL, OR THE RAJAH OF CHUTNEYPORE (Solomon) 22, 28, 41, 42

NAVARRAISE (Massenet) 01, 25, 32, 33, 34, 60, 64, 66

NAVE (Montemezzi) 73

NEBUCHADNEZZAR see NABUCCO

NELL GWYNNE (Planquette) 42

NELSON (Berkeley) 15, 16

NERO (Rubinstein) 10, 34

NERONE (Boito) 01, 15, 18, 40, 48, 64, 74

NERONE (Mascagni) 73

NEUES VOM TAGE (Hindemith) 15, 16, 25, 64, 69

NEW GIRL IN TOWN (Merrill) 29, 65

NEW MOON (Romberg) 22, 29, 41, 42

NEW WOMAN see FEMME NEU

NEWS OF THE DAY see NEUES VOM TAGE

NIGHT BELL see CAMPANELLO DI NOTTE

NIGHT FLIGHT see VOLO DI NOTTE

NIGHT IN MAY see MAY NIGHT

NIGHT IN VENICE see NACHT IN VENEDIG

NIGHTINGALE (Rogers) 24

NIGHTINGALE (Stravinsky) see ROSSIGNOL

NIGHT'S CAMP AT GRANADA see NACHTLAGER VON GRANADA

NINA, OSSIA, LA PAZZA PER AMORE (Paisiello) 25

NINE RIVERS FROM JORDAN (Weisgall) 23

NINETY-THREE (Silver) 73

NO, NO, NANETTE! (Youmans) 22, 29, 41, 42

NO STRINGS (Rodgers, R.) 29, 65

NOAH'S FLOOD see NOYE'S FLUDDE

NOCES DE JEANNETTE (Massé) 28, 34, 42

NOCES D'OLIVETTE (Audran) 28, 34, 41, 42

NORMA (Bellini) 01, 02, 03, 04, 08, 11, 12, 14, 15,
18, 19, 24, 27, 31, 32, 33, 34, 35, 36, 37, 39, 40, 42,
47, 48, 49, 57, 58, 60, 61, 62, 64, 66, 67, 68, 69, 70,
74; ON 18 #20; ON 34 #23; ON 35 #8-9; ON 37 #15; ON
40 #16

NOSE (Shostakovich) 25

NOTTE DI ZORAIMA (Montemezzi) 01, 73

NOYE'S FLUDDE (Britten) 24, 71, 74

NOZZE DI FIGARO (Mozart) 01, 02, 03, 04, 06, 07,
09, 11, 12, 14, 15, 18, 19, 20, 24, 26, 28, 30, 31, 32,
33, 34, 35, 36, 37, 39, 40, 42, 44, 45, 47, 48, 49, 50,
52, 54, 56, 57, 58, 60, 61, 62, 64, 66, 67, 68, 69, 70,
72, 74; ON 14 #15; ON 16 #17; ON 18 #7; ON 19 #10;
ON 20 #22; ON 22 #10; ON 24 #12; ON 25 #12; ON 29
#8; ON 32 #6; ON 34 #24; ON 40 #15

NUMBER 66 see SOIXANTE-SIX

NUREMBERG DOLL see POUPEE DE NUREMBERG

                              -O-

OATH see GUIRAMENTO

OBERON (Weber) 01, 02, 03, 04, 11, 15, 17, 19, 25,
32, 33, 34, 40, 42, 48, 60, 61, 62, 64, 66, 68, 69, 73,
74

OBERST CHABERT see COLONEL CHABERT

OBERSTEIGER (Zeller) 28

OCA DEL CAIRO (Mozart) 24

ODYSSEUS' RETURN (Bungert) 02

OEDIPUS (Enesco) 73

OEDIPUS REX (Stravinsky)   19, 24, 35, 36, 40, 48,
49, 69, 74

OF MICE AND MEN (Floyd)   25

OF THEE I SING! (Gershwin)   29, 41, 42

OH BOY! (Kern)   41

OH, KAY! (Gershwin)   29, 41, 42

OH! OH! DELPHINE (Caryll)   29, 42

OIE DU CAIRE see OCA DEL CAIRO

OISEAU BLEU (Wolff)   01, 32, 33, 42, 73

OKLAHOMA (Rodgers, R.)   22, 29, 41, 42, 65

OLD CHELSEA (Tauber)   22

OLD GUARD (Planquette)   41

OLD MAID AND THE THIEF (Menotti)   15, 16, 23, 24,
32, 33, 42, 48

OLD VIENNA see ALT WIEN

OLIVER (Bart)   65

OLIVETTE see NOCES D'OLIVETTE

OLYMPIANS (Bliss)   11, 15, 16

ON A CLEAR DAY YOU CAN SEE FOREVER (Lane)   29,
65

ON THE TOWN (Bernstein, L.)   29, 41

ON YOUR TOES (Rodgers, R.)   29, 41

ONCE UPON A MATTRESS (Rodgers, R.)   29, 65

ONE CHRISTMAS LONG AGO (Mayer) 25

110 IN THE SHADE (Schmidt) 29

ONE TOUCH OF VENUS (Weill) 29, 41

ONLY GIRL (Herbert) 29

OPENING (Wilder) 25

OPERA: ITALIAN STYLE see CONVENIENZE ED IN-
CONVENIENZE TEATRALE

OPERA OF ARAN (Bécaud) 25

OPERA, OPERA (Kalmanoff) 25

OPERAS-MINUTES see TROIS OPERAS MINUTES

OPERNBALL (Heuberger) 28, 41

OPRICHNIK (Chaikovskii) 10

ORACOLO (Leoni) 01, 32, 33, 42, 56, 60, 64, 66, 73

ORAZI ED I CURIAZI (Mercadante) MT 116 #1588 p.
555

ORCHID (Caryll & Monckton) 41

ORESTES (Křenek) 73

ORFEO (Monteverdi) see FAVOLA D'ORFEO

ORFEO E EURYDICE (Gluck) 01, 02, 03, 04, 07, 11,
12, 14, 15, 17, 19, 20, 24, 26, 32, 33, 34, 35, 36, 37,
39, 40, 42, 45, 48, 49, 50, 51, 57, 58, 60, 61, 62, 64,
66, 67, 68, 69, 71, 72, 74; ON 19 #22; ON 22 #11; ON
26 #17; ON 35 #11

ORMINDO (Cavalli) 25; JAMS 28 #2 p. 270, 282-3

ORPHEE AUX ENFERS (Offenbach) 19, 21, 24, 28, 34, 40, 41, 42, 49, 64, 66, 69, 74

ORPHEUS AND EURYDICE see ORFEO E EURYDICE

ORSEOLO (Pizzetti) 73

OSTERIA PORTOGHESE (Cherubini) 24

OSUD see FATE

OTELLO (Verdi) 01, 02, 03, 04, 06, 07, 08, 11, 12, 14, 15, 18, 19, 24, 25, 27, 30, 31, 32, 33, 34, 35, 36, 37, 39, 40, 42, 44, 45, 47, 48, 49, 50, 52, 55, 57, 58, 60, 61, 62, 64, 66, 67, 68, 69, 70, 73, 74; ON 16 #14; ON 19 #18; ON 22 #18; ON 23 #7; ON 27 #20; ON 28 #14; ON 31 #20; ON 36 #20; ON 37 #6; ON 38 #14

OTHER WISE MAN (Grove) 25

OTTONE (Handel) MT 112 #1544 p. 955-56

OUR MAN IN HAVANA (Williamson) 25

OUR MISS GIBBS (Caryll & Monckton) 22, 41

OUT OF THIS WORLD (Porter) 42

OUTCASTS OF POKER FLAT (Adler, S.) 25

OWEN WINGRAVE (Britten) 25, 74; ON 35 #27 p. 27; MT 112 #1539 p. 425

-P-

PADMAVATI (Roussel) 74

PADREVIA (Pastieri) 25

PAGANINI (Lehár) 21, 28, 41

PAGLIACCI (Leoncavallo) 01, 02, 03, 04, 06, 07, 09,
11, 12, 14, 15, 18, 19, 20, 24, 27, 30, 31, 32, 33, 34,
35, 36, 39, 40, 42, 45, 46, 47, 48, 49, 50, 51, 56, 57,
58, 60, 61, 62, 63, 64, 66, 67, 68, 69, 70, 74; ON 15
#19; ON 16 #12; ON 17 #22; ON 21 #22; On 23 #9; ON
24 #13; ON 27 #5; ON 28 #22; ON 34 #15; ON 35 #16;
ON 39 #11

PAILLASSE see PAGLIACCI

PAINT YOUR WAGON (Loewe) 29, 65

PAJAMA GAME (Adler, R. & Ross) 22, 29, 41, 65

PAL JOEY (Rodgers, R.) 29, 41, 65

PALESTRINA (Pfitzner) 32, 33, 40, 48, 64, 69, 74

PANAMA HATTIE (Porter) 29

PANTAGLEIZE (Starer) 25

PANTOMINES (Cole, B.) MT 113 #1547 p. 38

PARABLE FOR CHURCH PERFORMANCE see CURLEW
RIVER; BURNING FIERY FURNACE; PRODIGAL SON

PARDON OF PLOERMEL see DINORAH

PARDONER'S TALE (Sokoloff) 25

PARIDE E ELENA (Gluck) 64

PARISIAN LIFE see VIE PARISIENNE

PARISIAN MODEL (Hoffmann) 29

PARNASSO IN FESTA (Handel) MT 112 #1538 p. 339-40

PARSIFAL (Wagner, R.) 01, 02, 03, 04, 07, 09, 11, 12,
14, 15, 18, 19, 20, 24, 26, 30, 33, 34, 35, 36, 37, 39,
40, 42, 43, 44, 45, 47, 48, 49, 53, 56, 60, 61, 62, 64,
66, 67, 68, 69, 70, 72, 73, 74; ON 16 #23; ON 18 #23;
ON 20 #20; ON 24 #23; ON 30 #22; ON 35 #23; ON 38 #24

PASSING SHOW (Englander) 29

PASSION OF JONATHAN WADE (Carlisle) 23

PATIENCE (Sullivan) 04, 19, 28, 34, 41, 42, 66, 68

PATIENCE OF SOCRATES see GEDULTIGE SOCRATES

PAUL AND VIRGINIA (Gavazzeni) 73

PAUL AND VIRGINIA (Massé) 64

PAUL JONES (Planquette) 41

PAUVRE MATELOT (Milhaud) 15, 16, 24, 40, 48, 69, 73, 74

PEACE DAY see FRIEDENSTAG

PEARL FISHERS see PÊCHEURS DE PERLES

PEARL OF BRAZIL see PERLE DU BRESIL

PEARL OF PEKIN see FLEUR-DE-THE

PÊCHEURS DE PERLES (Bizet) 01, 04, 11, 12, 13, 15, 17, 19, 25, 32, 33, 40, 42, 48, 56, 60, 61, 64, 66, 67, 68, 73, 74

PEER GYNT (Egk) ON 30 #17 p. 32-33

PEGGY-ANN (Rodgers, R.) 29, 41

PELLEAS AND MELISANDE (Debussy) 01, 03, 04, 07, 08, 11, 12, 14, 15, 18, 19, 24, 27, 32, 33, 34, 35, 36, 39, 40, 42, 45, 47, 48, 49, 50, 51, 57, 58, 60, 61, 62, 64, 66, 67, 69, 70, 73, 74; ON 18 #8; ON 24 #11; ON 27 #8; ON 36 #10

PENELOPE (Fauré) 25, 74

PENELOPE (Liebermann) 69

PHILEMON AND BAUCIS (Gounod) 01, 02, 15, 18, 25, 32, 33, 64

PHILLIP MARSHALL (Barab) 25

PHOEBUS AND PAN see STREIT ZWISCHEN PHOEBUS UND PAN

PHOTOGRAPH-1920 (Kalmanoff) 25

PICCOLO MARAT (Mascagni) 73

PICNIC (Cumming) 25

PIERROT AND PIERRETTE see STRANGER

PIETRA DEL PARAGONE (Rossini) 25

PIFF, PAFF, POUF (Schwartz, J.) 29

PIKOVAYA DAMA see PIQUE DAME

PILATE (Hovhannes) 25

PILGRIM'S PROGRESS (Vaughan Williams) 11, 40, 48, 74

PILGRIMS TO MECCA see RECONTRE IMPREVUE

PIMPINONE (Telemann) 24

PINAFORE (Sullivan) 04, 19, 28, 34, 41, 42, 66, 68

PINK LADY (Caryll) 29, 41, 42

PIPE DREAM (Rodgers, R.) 29

PIPE OF DESIRE (Converse) 01, 32, 33, 42, 60, 64, 73

PIPER OF HAMELIN (Nessler) 01, 02, 42

PIQUE DAME (Chaikovskii) 01, 03, 04, 07, 10, 11, 12,

13, 15, 18, 19, 24, 32, 33, 39, 40, 42, 48, 49, 60, 61, 64, 66, 67, 68, 69, 70, 73, 74; ON 30 #11

PIRATA (Bellini) 25, 74

PIRATES OF PENZANCE (Sullivan) 04, 19, 28, 34, 41, 66, 68

PLAIN AND FANCY (Hague) 29, 41, 65

PLAYERS see PAGLIACCI

PLEDGE see BURGSCHAFT

PLOUGH AND THE STARS (Siegmeister) 25

POLENBLUT (Nedbal) 28

POACHER see WILDSCHUETZ

POISONED KISS (Vaughan Williams) 15, 18, 24, 40, 48, 74

POLISH JEW (Weiss) 73

POMO D'ORO (Cesti) JAMS 29, p. 383

POOR JONATHAN (Milloecker) 42

POOR SAILOR see PAUVRE MALELOT

POPPY (Jones, Stephen) 29

PORGY AND BESS (Gershwin) 04, 11, 13, 19, 23, 24, 29, 31, 32, 33, 39, 40, 42, 48, 61, 62, 65, 67, 69, 74

PORTRAIT DE MANON (Massenet) 24

PORTUGUESE INN see OSTERIA PORTOGHESE

POSTCARD FROM MOROCCO (Argento) 25

POSTILLON DE LONGJUMEAU (Adam) 01, 02, 25, 28, 32, 33, 34, 40, 42, 48, 60, 64, 69, 74

POT OF FAT (Chanler) 24

POTTER THOMPSON (Crosse) MT 116 #1585 p. 260

POULE NOIRE (Rosenthal) 25

POUPEE (Audran) 41

POUPEE DE NUREMBERG (Adam) 02, 28

POWER OF EVIL (Serov) 10

PRE AUX CLERCS (Hérold) 28

PRECIOSA (Weber) 01, 02

PRETENDING SIMPLETON see FINTA SEMPLIA

PRESENT ARMS (Rodgers, R.) 29

PRIDE OF THE REGIMENT, OR CASHIERED FOR HIS
COUNTRY (Leigh) 41

PRIGIONIERO (Dallapiccola) 24, 74

PRIHODY LISKY BYSTROUSKY see CUNNING LITTLE
VIXEN

PRIMA DONNA (Benjamin) 15, 16, 24

PRIMA LA MUSICA, POI LE PAROLE (Salieri) 25

PRINCE FERELON (Gatty) 15, 18

PRINCE IGOR (Borodin) 01, 03, 04, 07, 10, 11, 13,
15, 18, 19, 24, 32, 33, 35, 36, 40, 42, 48, 49, 51, 56,
60, 61, 62, 64, 66, 67, 68, 69, 70, 73, 74

PRINCE METHUSALEM (Strauss, J.) 41, 42

PRINCE OF PILSEN (Luders) 29, 41, 42

PRINCESS AND THE PEA (Toch) 24

P'TITES MICHU (Messager)   21, 41

PUNCH AND JUDY (Birtwistle)   25, 71

PURGATORY (Crosse)   25, 71

PURGATORY (Weisgall)   25

PURITANI (Bellini)   01, 13, 15, 18, 19, 25, 32, 33, 34, 40, 42, 48, 60, 61, 62, 64, 66, 67, 68, 69, 74; ON 40 #16

PURLIE (Geld)   29, 65

-Q-

QUAKER GIRL (Monckton)   22, 28, 41, 42

QUATRE JOURNEES (Bruneau)   73

QUATTRO RUSTEGHI (Wolf-Ferrari)   15, 16, 24, 28, 40, 48, 61, 69, 74

QUEEN HIGH (Gensler)   29

QUEEN OF CORNWALL (Boughton)   15, 18, 73

QUEEN OF HEARTS (Sousa)   05

QUEEN OF SHEBA (Goldmark)   01, 02, 15, 18, 32, 33, 34, 40, 48, 60, 64, 66, 68, 74

QUEEN OF SHEBA (Gounod)   see   REINE DE SABA

QUEEN OF SPADES   see   PIQUE-DAME

QUEEN TOPAZE   see   REINE TOPAZE

QUEEN'S HANDKERCHIEF   see   SPITZENTUCH DER KOENIGIN

RED HOT AND BLUE (Porter) 42

RED MILL (Herbert) 29, 41, 42

REDHEAD (Hague) 29, 65

REFORMED DRUNKARD see IVROGNE CORRIGE

REGINA (Blitzstein) 23, 29, 39, 45

REGINA DE SABA (Goldmark) see QUEEN OF SHEBA

REGINETTA DELLE ROSE (Leoncavallo) 01

REINE DE SABA (Gounod) 68

REINE FIAMETTA (Leroux) 01, 60, 73

REINE TOPAZE (Massé) 42

REMBRANDT VAN RIJN (Klenau) 73

RENARD (Stravinsky) 25, 28, 74

RENCONTRE IMPREVUE (Gluck) 28

RESURRECTION see RISURREZIONE

RETABLO DE MAESE PEDRO (Falla) 19, 24, 61, 74

REVE (Bruneau) 34

REVISOR (Egk) 69

REVOLUTIONSHOCHZEIT (Albert) 73

REWARD OF VIRTUE see BILLEE TAYLOR

RHEINGOLD (Wagner, R.) 01, 02, 03, 04, 07, 11, 12,
14, 15, 18, 19, 20, 24, 26, 30, 31, 32, 33, 34, 35,
36, 37, 39, 40, 42, 43, 45, 47, 48, 49, 53, 56, 57,
58, 60, 61, 62, 64, 66, 67, 68, 69, 72, 74; ON 15 #14;
ON 21 #11; ON 26 #5; ON 33 #17; ON 39 #15

RICH MR. HOGGENHEIMER (Englander) 29

RICHARD COEUR DE LION (Grêtry) 24

RIDERS TO THE SEA (Vaughan Williams) 24, 74

RIENZI (Wagner, R.) 01, 02, 03, 07, 19, 25, 32, 33, 34, 40, 42, 48, 60, 64, 66, 69, 74

RIGOLETTO (Verdi) 01, 02, 03, 04, 06, 07, 09, 11, 12, 14, 15, 18, 19, 20, 24, 27, 30, 31, 32, 33, 34, 35, 36, 37, 39, 40, 42, 45, 47, 48, 49, 50, 52, 55, 56, 57, 58, 60, 61, 62, 64, 66, 67, 68, 69, 70, 73, 74; ON 14 #18; ON 16 #5; ON 17 #18; ON 18 #5; ON 20 #16; ON 21 #8; ON 23 #21; ON 25 #8; ON 28 #15; ON 29 #5; ON 31 #24; ON 33 #6; ON 36 #11; ON 37 #14; ON 38 #8

RINALDO (Handel) 25, 68

RING DES NIBELUNGEN (Wagner, R.) 02, 03, 04, 07, 24, 26, 30, 31, 32, 33, 34, 35, 37, 40, 42, 45, 47, 48, 49, 56, 58, 60, 61, 62, 66, 67, 70, 72, 74. See also: GOETTERDAEMMERUNG; RHEINGOLD; SIEG-FRIED; WALKUERE

RIO RITA (Tierney) 29

RIP VAN WINKLE (Koven) 01, 32, 33, 42, 73

RIP VAN WINKLE (Planquette) 21, 41, 42

RISE AND FALL OF THE CITY OF MAHAGONNY (Weill) 25, 28, 74; ON 34 #20 p. 10

RISING OF THE MOON (Maw) 25

RISURREZIONE (Alfano) 66, 73

RITA (Donizetti) 24

RITORNO D'ULISSE IN PATRIA (Monteverdi) 40, 48, 74

RIVAL LOVERS see GOYESCAS

RIVERWIND (Jennings) 65

ROAR OF THE GREASEPAINT, THE SMELL OF THE
CROWD (Bricusse) 65

ROB ROY (Koven) 29, 42

ROBBERS (Rorem) 24

ROBERT LE DIABLE (Meyerbeer) 01, 02, 03, 04, 15,
18, 25, 32, 33, 34, 40, 42, 48, 60, 64, 66, 68, 74

ROBERTA (Kern) 29, 41, 42

ROBERTO DEVEREUX (Donizetti) 25, 74

ROBIN HOOD (Koven) 29, 34, 41, 42, 68

ROBIN WOMAN see SHANEWIS

ROBINSON CRUSOE, JR. (Romberg) 29

RODELINDA (Handel) 13, 15, 17, 25, 64, 69, 74

ROI CAROTTE (Offenbach) 41

ROI DE LAHORE see KING OF LAHORE

ROI D'YS (Lalo) 01, 19, 32, 33, 34, 40, 48, 60, 64,
68, 73, 74

ROI L'A DIT (Delibes) 01, 02, 28

ROI MALGRE LUI see KING AGAINST HIS WILL

ROLANDE ET LE MAUVAIS GARÇON (Rabaud) 73

ROMEO ET JULIETTE (Gounod) 01, 02, 03, 04, 12, 14,
15, 18, 19, 24, 27, 32, 33, 34, 40, 42, 47, 48, 51, 60,
61, 62, 64, 66, 67, 68, 70, 74; ON 32 #24; ON 34 #25;
ON 37 #21; ON 39 #6

ROMEO UND JULIA (Blacher) 25

ROMEO UND JULIA AUF DEM DORF see VILLAGE
ROMEO AND JULIET

RONDINE (Puccini) 01, 04, 13, 25, 32, 33, 40, 42, 48,
60, 64, 66, 67, 73, 74

ROOM NO. 12 (Kanitz) 25

ROPE (Mennini) 24

ROSALIE (Gershwin) 29

ROSALINDA (Strauss, J.) 42

ROSAURA see EQUIVOCI IN AMORE

ROSE MARIE (Friml & Stothart) 22, 29, 41, 42

ROSE OF ALGERIA (Herbert) 42

ROSE OF PERSIA (Sullivan) 22

ROSE VON STAMBUL (Fall) 41

ROSENKAVALIER (Strauss, R.) 01, 03, 04, 07, 09, 11, 12,
14, 15, 18, 19, 24, 26, 30, 31, 32, 33, 35, 36, 39, 40, 42,
44, 45, 46, 47, 48, 49, 50, 51, 56, 57, 58, 60, 61, 62, 64,
66, 67, 69, 70, 72, 73, 74; ON 14 #5; ON 15 #18; ON 17
#17; ON 20 #15; ON 22 #20; ON 24 #8; ON 27 #7; ON 29 #6;
ON 33 #15; ON 34 #18; ON 37 #23; ON 38 #16; ON 40 #18

ROSINDA (Cavalli) MT 114 #1560 p. 133

ROSSIGNOL (Stravinsky) 01, 15, 18, 25, 32, 33, 40,
42, 48, 60, 61, 64, 66, 69, 73, 74

ROUND ABOUT PARNASSUS see AMFIPARNASO

ROYAL AUCTION (Kanitz) 25

ROYAL CHILDREN see KOENIGSKINDER

ROYAL HUNT OF THE SUN (Hamilton) 25

ROYALTY AND ROGUERY see QUEEN OF HEARTS

RUBY (Dello Joio) 24, 33

RUDDIGORE (Sullivan) 04, 19, 28, 41, 42

RUNAWAY GIRL (Caryll & Monckton) 28, 41, 42

RUNAWAYS (Hubbell) 29

RUSALKA (Dvorak) 15, 18, 25, 64, 74

RUSALKA (Dargomijsky) 01, 10

RUSSLAN AND LUDMILLA (Glinka) 01, 04, 10, 19, 25, 32, 33, 40, 42, 48, 64, 74

RUSTIC CHIVALRY see CAVALLERIA RUSTICANA

RUTH (Berkeley) 71

-S-

SACK OF CALABASAS (Fletcher) 25

SACRED MOUNTAIN see HEILIGE BERG

SACRIFICE (Converse) 01, 42, 73

SADKO (Rimskii-Korsakov) 01, 04, 10, 15, 18, 19, 25, 32, 33, 40, 42, 48, 49, 60, 61, 64, 73, 74

SAINT ELIZABETH see LEGENDE VON DER HEILIGEN ELISABETH

SAINT LOUIS WOMAN (Arlen) 29

SAINT OF BLEECKER STREET (Menotti) 14, 15, 16, 23, 24, 33, 39, 61, 69, 74

SERENADE (Herbert) 29, 42

SERF (Lloyd) 15, 18

SERSE (Handel) 03, 60, 64

SERVA PADRONA (Pergolesi) 15, 17, 24, 25, 28, 32,
33, 39, 40, 42, 48, 60, 61, 62, 64, 67, 69, 73, 74

SERVANT MISTRESS see SERVA PADRONA

SERVANT OF TWO MASTERS (Stambler) 23

SETTE CANZONI (Malipiero) 60, 64

SEVENTEEN DAYS AND FOUR MINUTES see SIEB-
ZEHN TAGE UND 4 MINUTEN

1776 (Edwards) 29, 65

SHAMUS O'BRIEN (Stanford) 15, 18, 34, 73

SHANEWIS (Cadman) 01, 32, 33, 42, 60, 64, 66, 73

SHARPSHOOTER see FREISCHUETZ

SHE LOVES ME (Bock) 29, 65

SHEPHERDS OF THE DELECTABLE MOUNTAINS (Vaughan Williams) 24

SHINING CHALICE (Grove) 25

SHIP see NAVE

SHO-GUN (Luders) 29, 42

SHOEMAKER'S HOLIDAY (Argento) 25

SHOP GIRL (Caryll) 22, 41

SHORT LIFE see VIDA BREVE

SHOW BOAT (Kern) 22, 29, 41, 42, 65

SHOW GIRL (Gershwin) 29

SI J'ETAIS ROI (Adam) 28

SIBERIA (Giordano) 01, 73

SICILIAN VESPERS see VESPRI SICILIANI

SIEBZEHN TAGE UND 4 MINUTEN (Egk) 25

SIEGE OF CORINTH see ASSEDIO DI CORINTO

SIEGFRIED (Wagner, R.) 01, 02, 03, 04, 07, 11, 12,
14, 15, 18, 19, 20, 24, 26, 30, 31, 32, 33, 34, 35,
36, 37, 39, 40, 42, 43, 45, 47, 48, 49, 53, 56, 57,
58, 60, 61, 62, 64, 66, 67, 68, 69, 72, 74; ON 15 #16;
ON 21 #14; ON 26 #9; ON 39 #15

SIGNOR BRUSCHINO (Rossini) 25, 28, 60, 64, 73

SIGURD (Reyer) 34

SILENT WOMAN see SCHWEIGSAME FRAU

SILK STOCKINGS (Porter) 29, 65

SILVANA (Weber) 01, 02

SIMON BOCCANEGRA (Verdi) 01, 03, 04, 08, 11, 12,
14, 15, 17, 19, 24, 32, 33, 35, 36, 37, 39, 40, 42, 45,
48, 49, 60, 61, 62, 64, 67, 69, 70, 73, 74; ON 14 #13;
ON 24 #22; ON 25 #15; ON 29 #12; ON 33 #7; ON 38
#11

SIMPLE SIMON (Rodgers, R.) 29

SIMPLICIUS (Strauss, J.) 41

SINBAD (Romberg) 29

SIR JOHN IN LOVE (Vaughan Williams) 24

SOMEBODY'S SWEETHEART (Bafunno) 29

SOMETHING FOR THE BOYS (Porter) 29

SOMETIME (Friml) 29

SON BY CHANCE see SIGNOR BRUSCHINO

SONG OF FORTUNIO see CHANSON DE FORTUNIO

SONG OF NORWAY (Grieg; arr. Wright & Forrest) 29, 41, 42, 65

SONG OF THE FLAME (Gershwin & Stothart) 29

SONGSTRESS see CANTERINA

SONNAMBULA (Bellini) 01, 02, 03, 04, 11, 14, 15, 18, 19, 24, 27, 32, 33, 34, 35, 36, 37, 39, 40, 42, 48, 49, 60, 61, 64, 66, 67, 68, 69, 73, 74; ON 27 #21; ON 33 #8

SONS O'GUNS (Coots) 29

SOPHIE ARNOULD (Pierné) 25

SORCERER (Sullivan) 04, 19, 28, 34, 41, 42

SORCERESS (Chaikovskii) 10

SOROCHINSKAYA YARMARKA see FAIR AT SOROCHIN-TZKY

SORROWS OF ORPHEUS see MALHEURS D'ORPHEE

SOSARME (Handel) 19

SOTOBA KOMACHI (Levy, M.) 24

SOUND OF MUSIC (Rodgers, R.) 22, 29, 41, 65

SOURWOOD MOUNTAIN (Kreutz) 25

SOUTH PACIFIC (Rodgers, R.) 22, 29, 41, 42, 65

SPANISH HOUR see HEURE ESPAGNOLE

SPEZIALE (Haydn) 01, 02, 24, 28, 39

SPIRIT OF OLD VIENNA see WIENER BLUT

SPITZENTUCH DER KOENIGIN (Strauss, J.) 28, 34, 41, 42, 66. (Adapted by Karl Pauspertl - 41, 66)

SPLIT PERSONALITY see ZERRISSENE

SPRING MAIDEN see SUESSE MAEDEL

SPUK IM SCHLOSS (Křička) 73

STAG KING see KOENIG HIRSCH

STANDRECHT see WRECKERS

STAR OF THE NORTH see ETOILE DU NORD

STEPPING STONES (Kern) 29

STERLINGMANN, OR, GENEROSITY REWARDED (Roy) 25

STIFFELIO (Verdi) MT 114 #1562 p. 398

STONE GUEST (Dargomijsky) 10, 15, 18, 60, 64

STOP! LOOK! LISTEN! (Berlin) 29

STOP THE WORLD - I WANT TO GET OFF (Bricusse) 65

STORY OF TSAR SULTAN see TSAR SULTAN

STORY OF VASCO (Crosse) MT 115 #1575 p. 403

STRADELLA see ALESSANDRO STRADELLA

TALES OF HOFFMANN (Offenbach) 01, 03, 04, 07, 08,
11, 12, 14, 15, 18, 19, 24, 27, 30, 32, 33, 34, 35, 36,
39, 40, 42, 47, 48, 49, 52, 55, 56, 57, 58, 60, 61, 62,
64, 66, 67, 68, 69, 70, 73, 74; ON 20 #4; ON 21 #6;
ON 23 #14; ON 29 #16; ON 35 #24; ON 38 #13

TAMERLANO (Handel) 03, 25, 60

TAMING OF THE SHREW (Gianini) 23, 24, 33, 45

TAMING OF THE SHREW (Goetz) 01, 02, 34, 64, 69

TANCREDI (Rossini) MT 112 #1538 p. 326

TANGERINE (Sanders) 29

TANNHAUSER (Wagner, R.) 01, 02, 03, 04, 06, 07,
09, 11, 12, 14, 15, 18, 19, 20, 24, 26, 30, 31, 32, 33,
34, 35, 36, 37, 39, 40, 42, 43, 45, 47, 48, 49, 53, 56,
57, 58, 60, 61, 62, 64, 66, 67, 68, 69, 70, 72, 74; ON
18 #9; ON 19 #12; ON 25 #6; ON 30 #21

TANTIVY TOWERS (Dunhill) 41

TANZ INS GLUECK (Stolz) 41

TAPFERE SOLDAT see CHOCOLATE SOLDIER

TARA'S FAMILY see FAMILY OF TARAS

TARTAJARAS (Kálmán) 41

TARTUFFE (Haug) 73

TAVERNER (Davies, P.) 25; MT 113 #1555 p. 879

TCHEREVICHKI see CHEREVICHKY

TEDIOUS WAY TO THE PLACE OF NATASCHA UNGE-
HEUER see LANGWIERIGE WEG IN DIE WOHNUNG
DER NATASCHA UNGEHEUER

TELEPHONE (Menotti) 11, 15, 16, 24, 32, 33, 40, 42,
45, 61, 62, 74

THREE WALTZES see DREI WALZER

THREE WISHES see TROIS SOUHAITS

THROUGH THE YEARS (Youmans) 42

TICKLE ME (Stothart) 29

TIDE see FLUT

TIEFLAND (Albert) 01, 25, 32, 33, 40, 42, 48, 60, 64, 66, 69, 73, 74

TIME OFF? NOT A GHOST OF A CHANCE! (Lutyens) MT 113 #1550 p. 376

TIP-TOES (Gershwin) 29

TIRESIAS see MAMELLES DE TIRESIAS

TOBIAS WUNDERLICH (Haas) 69

TODT STADT see TOTE STADT

TOEDLICHEN WUENSCHE (Klebe) 69

TOLOMEO (Handel) MT 114 #1569 p. 1154

TOM JONES (German) 22, 28, 41, 42

TOP BANANA (Mercer) 29

TOREADOR (Caryll & Monckton) 22, 41

TORQUATO TASSO (Donizetti) MT 115 #1574 p. 319-20

TOSCA (Puccini) 01, 03, 04, 06, 07, 09, 11, 12, 14, 15, 18, 19, 24, 27, 30, 31, 32, 33, 34, 35, 36, 39, 40, 42, 44, 45, 46, 47, 48, 49, 50, 52, 55, 56, 57, 58, 60, 61, 62, 64, 66, 67, 68, 69, 70, 73, 74; ON 14 #12; ON 17 #6; ON 20 #9; ON 21 #19; ON 22 #19; ON 23 #23; ON 24 #20; ON 26 #21; ON 28 #23; ON 29 #23; ON 32 #11; ON 33 #16; ON 34 #11; ON 35 #7; ON 39 #14

TOTE STADT (Korngold) 01, 25, 32, 33, 42, 60, 64, 73

TOTEN AUGEN (Albert) 25

TOUCHSTONE see PIETRA DEL PARAGONE

TOWER (Levy, M.) 24

TRAGEDY IN AREZZO see CAPONSACCHI

TRANSPOSED HEADS (Glanville-Hicks) 25

TRAUM DES LIU-TUNG (Yun) 25

TRAVELLING COMPANION (Stanford) 07, 15, 18, 73

TRAVIATA (Verdi) 01, 02, 03, 04, 06, 07, 09, 11, 12, 14, 15, 18, 19, 20, 24, 27, 30, 31, 32, 33, 34, 35, 36, 37, 39, 40, 42, 44, 45, 46, 47, 48, 49, 50, 52, 55, 56, 57, 58, 60, 61, 62, 63, 64, 66, 67, 68, 69, 70, 74; ON 15 #6; ON 16 #4; ON 18 #13; ON 19 #8; ON 21 #21; ON 22 #16; ON 23 #12; ON 26 #23; ON 27 #19; ON 28 #9; ON 31 #22; ON 32 #9; ON 34 #21; ON 37 #10; ON 40 #14

TREE ON THE PLAINS (Bacon) 24

TREES GROW IN BROOKLYN (Schwartz, A.) 29

TRIAL see PROZESS

TRIAL BY JURY (Sullivan) 04, 19, 28, 41, 42

TRIAL OF MARY LINCOLN (Pasatieri) 25; ON 36 #14 p. 32

TRILOGY: THE CAULDRON OF ANNWN see BRON-WEN; CHILDREN OF DON; DYLAN, SON OF THE WAVE

TRIONFO DELL'ONORE (Scarlatti, A.) 24

TRIP TO CHINATOWN (Grant) 29

TRISTAN UND ISOLDE (Wagner, R.)   01, 02, 03, 04,
06, 07, 09, 11, 12, 14, 15, 18, 19, 20, 24, 26, 30,
31, 32, 33, 34, 35, 36, 37, 39, 40, 42, 45, 46, 47,
49, 52, 53, 56, 57, 58, 60, 61, 62, 64, 66, 67, 68,
69, 70, 72, 73, 74; ON 14 #7; ON 15 #7; ON 17 #20;
ON 19 #19; ON 22 #17; ON 24 #10; ON 25 #19; ON 27
#16; ON 36 #5; ON 38 #12

TRITTICO see GIANNI SCHICCHI; SUOR ANGELICA;
TABARRO

TRIUMPH OF HONOR see TRIONFO DELL'ONORE

TRIUMPH OF ST. JOAN (Dello Joio) 23, 39

TROILUS AND CRESSIDA (Walton) 11, 15, 16, 24, 33,
45, 61, 74

TROIS OPERAS-MINUTES (Milhaud) 25, 40, 74

TROIS SOUHAITS (Martinu) MT 112 #1542 p. 780

TROJANS see TROYENS

TROUBADOUR see TROVATORE

TROUBLE IN TAHITI (Bernstein, L.) 24, 45

TROUBLED ISLAND (Still) 23

TROVATORE (Verdi) 01, 02, 03, 04, 06, 07, 09, 11,
12, 14, 15, 18, 19, 20, 24, 27, 30, 31, 32, 34, 35, 36
37, 39, 40, 42, 43, 45, 46, 47, 48, 49, 50, 52, 55, 56
57, 58, 60, 61, 62, 64, 66, 67, 68, 69, 70, 74; ON 15
#12; ON 18 #10; ON 20 #23; ON 21 #18; ON 24 #17; ON
25 #13; ON 28 #10; ON 30 #5; ON 31 #17; ON 33 #22;
ON 35 #20; ON 37 #19

TROYENS (Berlioz) 01, 03, 07, 13, 15, 17, 19, 25, 34
35, 36, 37, 40, 42, 48, 49, 51, 60, 61, 62, 64, 67, 69
74; ON 31 #4; ON 38 #19

TRUMPETER OF SAEKKINGEN (Nessler) 01, 02, 32,
33, 34, 42, 64

TSAR AND CARPENTER see ZAR UND ZIMMERMANN

TSAR SULTAN see LEGEND OF TSAR SULTAN

TSAR'S BRIDE (Rimskii-Korsakov) 10, 25, 60, 73

TURANDOT (Busoni) 25, 40, 48, 74

TURANDOT (Puccini) 01, 03, 04, 11, 12, 14, 15, 18,
19, 24, 32, 33, 35, 36, 39, 40, 42, 44, 45, 46, 48, 49,
50, 51, 58, 60, 61, 62, 64, 66, 67, 69, 70, 73, 74; ON
25 #17; ON 26 #15; ON 29 #10; ON 31 #6; ON 33 #21;
ON 34 #17; ON 38 #24; ON 39 #9

TURCO IN ITALIA (Rossini) 15, 17, 24, 28, 61, 74

TURN OF THE SCREW (Britten) 19, 24, 33, 45, 49,
69, 71, 74

TWELFTH NIGHT (Amram) 25

TWILIGHT OF THE GODS see GOETTERDAMMERUNG

TWO FOSCARI see DUE FOSCARI

TWO GRENADIERS (Lortzing) 02

TWO HEARTS IN THREE-QUARTER TIME see ZWEI
HERZEN IM DREIVIERTELTAKT

TWO LITTLE GIRLS IN BLUE (Youmans & Lannin) 29

TWO MISERS see DEUX AVARES

TWO WIDOWS see DVE VDOVY

-U-

UNDINE (Lortzing) 01, 02, 28, 42

UNICORN, THE GORGON AND THE MANTICORE (Menotti) 33

VIOLANTE (Korngold) 66, 73

VIOLINS OF SAINT JACQUES (Williamson) 25

VISION OF THERESE (Werle) MT 115 #1580 p. 867

VISIT OF THE OLD LADY see BESUCH DER ALTEN
DAME

VISITORS (Gardner) MT 113 #1554 p. 796

VIVANDIERE (Godard) 01

VOGELHAENDLER (Zeller) 21, 28, 41, 69

VOICE OF ARIADNE (Musgrave) MT 115 #1576 p. 465;
MT 115 #1578 p. 678

VOICE OF NATURE see POACHER

VOIX HUMAINE (Poulenc) 25, 45, 67

VOLO DI NOTTE (Dallapiccola) 25

VON HEUTE AUF MORGEN (Schoenberg) 74

VYLETY PANĚ BROUČKOVY see EXCURSIONS OF
MR. BROUCEK

-W-

WAFFENSCHMIED (Lortzing) 01, 02, 25, 28, 42

WALD see FOREST

WALKING HAPPY (Heusen) 65

WALKUERE (Wagner, R.) 01, 02, 03, 04, 06, 07, 11,
12, 14, 15, 18, 19, 20, 24, 26, 30, 31, 32, 33, 34, 35,
36, 37, 39, 40, 42, 43, 45, 47, 48, 49, 53, 56, 57, 58,
60, 61, 62, 64, 66, 67, 68, 69, 72, 74; ON 14 #20; ON

WHAT					121

WHAT MAKES SAMMY RUN? (Drake) 29

WHAT MEN LIVE BY (Martinu) 24

WHAT PRICE CONFIDENCE (Křenek) 25

WHERE'S CHARLEY? (Loesser) 29, 65

WHIRLPOOL (Suchon) 25

WHITE HORSE INN see IM WEISSEN ROESSL

WHITE LADY see DAME BLANCHE

WHITE WINGS (Moore) 25

WHOOPEE (Donaldson) 29

WHO'S THE BROTHER? WHO'S THE SISTER? (Verstovsky) 10

WIDERSPAENSTIGEN ZAEHMUNG see TAMING OF THE SHREW

WIENER BLUT (Strauss, J.) 21, 28, 41, 61, 69, 74

WIENER FRAUEN (Lehár) 41

WIFE OF MARTIN GUERRE (Bergsma) 24

WILDCAT (Coleman) 29, 65

WILDFLOWER (Youmans & Stothart) 29

WILDSCHUETZ (Lortzing) 01, 02, 25, 28, 40, 48, 69, 74

WILL-O'-THE-WISP see IRRLICHT

WILLIAM TELL (Rossini) 01, 02, 03, 04, 07, 15, 17, 19, 25, 27, 32, 33, 34, 40, 42, 48, 54, 60, 61, 62, 64, 66, 67, 69, 74

122

Title Index

WILLIS see VILLI

WINGS OF THE DOVE (Moore) 23, 25

WISE WOMAN AND THE KING see KLUGE

WISH YOU WERE HERE (Rome) 29, 41, 65

WITCH OF SALEM (Cadman) 32, 33, 42, 73

WITWE DES SCHMETTERLINGS (Yun) 25

WIZARD see ENCHANTER

WIZARD MILLER, CHEAT AND MARRIAGE BROKER
(Fomin) 10

WIZARD OF BALIZAR (Lockwood) 25

WIZARD OF OZ (Sloane & Tietjens) 29, 41

WIZARD OF THE NILE (Herbert) 29, 42

WO DIE LERCHE SINGT (Lehár) 41

WOLF (Sousa) 05

WOMAN WITHOUT A KISS see FRAU OHNE KUSS

WOMAN WITHOUT A SHADOW see FRAU OHNE
SCHATTEN

WOMEN (Pasatieri) 25

WONDERFUL TOWN (Bernstein, L.) 29, 41, 65

WOODLAND (Luders) 42

WORLD IS BEAUTIFUL see SCHOEN IST DIE WELT

WORLD OF THE MOON see MONDO DELLA LUNA

WOZZECK (Berg) 03, 11, 14, 15, 16, 24, 31, 32, 33, 35, 36, 39, 40, 42, 48, 49, 50, 51, 58, 60, 61, 62, 64, 67, 69, 73, 74; ON 23 #19; ON 25 #22; ON 33 #24

WRECKERS (Smyth) 07, 15, 18, 40, 48, 64, 74

WUNDERTHEATER (Henze) 25

WUTHERING HEIGHTS (Floyd) 23, 24

-X-

XERXES see SERSE

-Y-

YEOMAN OF THE GUARD (Sullivan) 04, 19, 28, 34, 41, 42

YERMA (Villa-Lobos) 25

YEVGENY ONYEGIN see EUGENE ONEGIN

YOLIMBA, ODER DIE GRENZEN DER MAGIE (Killmayer) 25

YOUNG ENGLAND (Clutsam & Bath) 41

YOUNG LORD see JUNGE LORD

YOUR OWN THING (Hester & Apolinar) 29, 65

YOUR REPUTATION DEPENDS ON HOW YOU LIVE (Matinsky) 10

YOU'RE A GOOD MAN CHARLIE BROWN (Gesner) 29, 65

-Z-

PART III

Composer Index

COMPOSER INDEX

-A-

Abraham, Paul
VICTORIA UND IHR
HUSAR

Adam, Adolphe Charles
POSTILLON DE LONG-
JUMEAU
POUPEE DE NUREM-
BERG
SI J'ETAIS ROI

Adler, Richard
DAMN YANKEES (with J.
Ross)
PAJAMA GAME (with J.
Ross)

Adler, Samuel
OUTCASTS OF POKER
FLAT

Ager, Milton
RAIN OR SHINE (with O.
Murphy)

Albert, Eugene d'
MISTER WU
REVOLUTIONSHOCHZEIT
TIEFLAND
TOTEN AUGEN

Alfano, Franco
CYRANO DE BERGERAC
MADAME IMPERIA
RISURREZIONE

Amram, David
TWELFTH NIGHT

Anderson, Leroy
GOLDILOCKS

Antheil, George
HELEN RETIRES

Apolinar, Danny
YOUR OWN THING
(with H. Hester)

Archer, Harry
LITTLE JESSIE
JAMES

Arensky, Antony S.
RAFAEL

Argento, Dominick
BOOR
CHRISTOPHER SLY
COLONEL JONATHAN
THE SAINT
MASQUE OF ANGELS
POSTCARD FROM
MOROCCO
SHOEMAKER'S HOLI-
DAY

Arlen, Harold
BLOOMER GIRL
HOORAY FOR WHAT?
HOUSE OF FLOWERS
JAMAICA
LIFE BEGINS AT 8:40

127

Bécaud, Gilbert
  OPERA OF ARAN

Becker, Reinhold
  FRAUENLOB

Beeson, Jack
  HELLO OUT THERE
  MY HEART'S IN THE
    HIGHLAND
  SWEET BYE-AND-BYE

Beethoven, Ludwig van
  FIDELIO

Bellini, Vincenzo
  BEATRICE DI TENDA
  CAPULETI E I MONTEC-
    CHI
  NORMA
  PIRATA
  PURITANI
  SONNAMBULA
  STRANIERA

Benatzky, Ralph
  IM WEISSEN ROESSL
  LIEBE IM SCHNEE
  MEINE SCHWESTER UND
    ICH

Benedict, Julius
  LILY OF KILLARNEY

Benjamin, Arthur
  DEVIL TAKE HER
  PRIMA DONNA
  TALE OF TWO CITIES

Bennett, Robert Russell
  CARMEN JONES (ar-
    rangement of Bizet's
    CARMEN)
  LEDGE
  MINES OF SULPHUR
  MARIA MALIBRAN

Berg, Alban
  LULU
  WOZZECK

Bergsma, William
  WIFE OF MARTIN
    GUERRE

Berkeley, Lennox
  CASTAWAY
  DINNER ENGAGEMENT
  NELSON
  RUTH

Berlin, Irving
  ANNIE GET YOUR GUN
  AS THOUSANDS CHEER
  CALL ME MADAM
  COCOANUTS
  FACE THE MUSIC
  LOUISIANA PURCHASE
  MISS LIBERTY
  MISTER PRESIDENT
  STOP! LOOK! LISTEN!

Berlioz, Hector
  BEATRICE ET BENE-
    DICT
  BENVENUTO CELLINI
  DAMNATION OF FAUST
  TROYENS

Berners, Gerald Hugh
  CARROSSE DU SAINT-
    SACRAMENT

Bernstein, Elmer
  HOW NOW, DOW
    JONES

Bernstein, Leonard
  CANDIDE
  ON THE TOWN
  TROUBLE IN TAHITI
  WEST SIDE STORY
  WONDERFUL TOWN

STOP THE WORLD - I
WANT TO GET OFF

Britten, Benjamin
ALBERT HERRING
BILLY BUDD
BURNING FIERY FUR-
NACE
CURLEW RIVER
DEATH IN VENICE
GLORIANA
LET'S MAKE AN OPERA
MIDSUMMER NIGHT'S
DREAM
NOYE'S FLUDDE
OWEN WINGRAVE
PETER GRIMES
PRODIGAL SON
RAPE OF LUCRETIA
TURN OF THE SCREW

Brooks, Richard
RAPUNZEL

Brown, Oscar, Jr.
JOY

Brüll, Ignaz
GOLDEN CROSS

Bruneau, Alfred
ATTAQUE DU MOULIN
QUATRE JOURNEES
REVE

Bucci, Mark
DRESS
TALE FOR A DEAR EAR

Bungert, August
ODYSSEUS' RETURN

Bush, Alan
WAT TYLER

Bush, Geoffrey
LORD ARTHUR SAVILE'S
CRIME

Busoni, Ferruccio
ARLECCHINO
DOKTOR FAUST
TURANDOT

-C-

Cadman, Charles Wakefield
SHANEWIS
WITCH OF SALEM

Caldwell, Mary E.
GIFT OF SONG

Canonica, Pietro
MIRANDA

Carmines, Al
PROMENADE

Carroll, Earl
EARL CARROLL'S VAN-
ITIES

Caryll, Ivan
CHIN-CHIN
CIRCUS GIRL
DUCHESS OF DANTZIC
EARL AND THE GIRL
MESSENGER BOY (with
L. Monckton)
OH! OH! DELPHINE
ORCHID (with L. Monck-
ton)
OUR MISS GIBBS (with
L. Monckton)
PINK LADY
RUNAWAY GIRL (with
L. Monckton)
SHOP GIRL
TOREADOR (with L.
Monckton)

Casella, Alfredo
FAVOLA DI ORFEO
GIARA
DONNA SERPENTE

Catalani, Alfredo
    LORELEY
    WALLY

Cavalli, Francesco
    CALISTO
    ERISMENA
    GIASONE
    ORMINDO
    ROSINDA

Cellier, Alfred
    DOROTHY
    MOUNTEBANKS

Cesti, Antonio
    POMO D'ORO

Chabrier, Alexis E.
    EDUCATION MANQUEE
    ETOILE
    GWENDOLINE
    KING AGAINST HIS WILL

Chaikovskii, Petr Il'ich
    CHEREVICHKI
    EUGENE ONEGIN
    IOLANTA
    MAID OF ORLEANS
    MAZEPPA
    OPRICHNIK
    PIQUE DAME
    SORCERESS

Chanler, Theodor
    POT OF FAT

Charig, Phil
    FOLLOW THE GIRLS

Charlap, Mark
    PETER PAN

Charpentier, Gustave
    JULIEN
    LOUISE

Chassaigne, Francis
    FALKA

Cherubini, Luigi
    DEUX JOURNEES
    MEDEE
    OSTERIA PORTOGHESE

Christine, Henri
    PHI-PHI

Cilea, Francesco
    ADRIANA LECOUVREUR
    ARLESIANA

Cimarosa, Domenico
    MATRIMONIO SEGRETO

Clarke, Henry Leland
    LOAFER AND THE
    LOAF

Clutsam, George H.
    YOUNG ENGLAND (with
    H. Bath)

Cockshott, Gerald
    APOLLO AND PERSE-
    PHONE
    FAUN IN THE FOREST

Cohan, George
    FORTY-FIVE MINUTES
    FROM BROADWAY
    GEORGE M!
    GEORGE WASHINGTON,
    JR.
    LITTLE JOHNNY JONES
    LITTLE MILLIONAIRE

Cole, Bruce
    HARLEQUINADE PAN-
    TOMINES

Coleman, Cy
    LITTLE ME

SWEET CHARITY
WILDCAT

Converse, Frederick
PIPE OF DESIRE
SACRIFICE

Coots, J. Fred
ARTISTS AND MODELS
(with S. Romberg)
SALLY, IRENE, AND
MARY
SONS O'GUNS

Copland, Aaron
TENDER LAND

Cornelius, Peter
BARBER OF BAGDAD

Courtney, C. C.
SALVATION (with P.
Link)

Coward, Noël
BITTER SWEET
CONVERSATION PIECE

Cremesini, Mario
FIERA

Crosse, Gordon
GRACE OF TODD
POTTER THOMPSON
PURGATORY
STORY OF VASCO

Crowne, John
CALISTO

Cui, César
MADEMOISELLE FIFI

Cumming, Richard
PICNIC

Cuvillier, Charles
LILA DOMINO

-D-

D'Albert see Albert

Dallapiccola, Luigi
PRIGIONIERO
VOLO DI NOTTE

Damrosch, Walter Johannes
CYRANO DE BERGERAC
MAN WITHOUT A COUN-
TRY
SCARLET LETTER

Dargomijsky, Aleksandr
RUSALKA
STONE GUEST

Darnley, Herbert
MR. WIX OF WICKHAM

David, Felicien
PERLE DU BRESIL

Davies, Harry Parr
LISBON STORY

Davies, Peter Maxwell
EIGHT SONGS FOR A
MAD KING
TAVERNER

DeBréville, Pierre see
Bréville

Debussy, Claude
ENFANT PRODIGUE
MARTYRE DE SAINT
SEBASTIAN
PELLEAS AND MELI-
SANDE

DeKoven see Koven

Delibes, Leo
COPPELIA
LAKME
ROI L'A DIT

Delius, Frederick
   IRMELIN
   KOANGA
   MAGIC FOUNTAIN
   VILLAGE ROMEO AND
      JULIET

Dello Joio, Norman
   RUBY
   TRIUMPH OF ST. JOAN

DePaul, Gene
   LI'L ABNER

D'Erlanger see Erlanger

Dessau, Paul
   LANZELOT

Dibdin, Charles
   EPHESIAN MATRON

Dittersdorf, Karl Ditters von
   DOCTOR AND THE
      APOTHECARY

Donaldson, Walter
   WHOOPEE

Donizetti, Gaetano
   ALAHOR IN GRANATA
   ANNA BOLENA
   BELISAIRE
   CAMPANELLO DI NOTTE
   CATERINA CORNARO
   CONVENIENZE ED IN-
      CONVENIENZE
      TEATRALE
   DON PASQUALE
   ELISIR D'AMORE
   FAVORITA
   FIGLIA DEL REGGIMEN-
      TO
   LINDA DI CHAMOUNIX
   LUCIA DI LAMMERMOOR
   LUCREZIA BORGIA
   MARIA PADILLA

   MARIA STUARDA
   RITA
   ROBERTO DEVEREUX
   TORQUATO TASSO

Dougherty, Celius
   MANY MOONS

Draeseke, Felix
   HERRAT

Drake, Ervin
   WHAT MAKES SAMMY
      RUN?

Dukas, Paul
   ARIANE ET BARBE
      BLEUE

Duke, Vernon
   BANJO EYES
   CABIN IN THE SKY

Dunhill, Thomas F.
   TANTIVY TOWERS

Dvorak, Antonin
   ALFRED
   ARMIDA
   DEVIL AND KATE
   JACOBIN
   RUSALKA

                -E-

Eaton, John
   HERACLES

Edwards, Julian
   DOLLY VARDEN

Edwards, Sherman
   1776

Egk, Werner
   COLUMBUS

IRISCHE LEGENDE
PEER GYNT
REVISOR
SIEBZEHN TAGE UND 4
  MINUTEN
ZAUBERGEIGE

Einem, Gottfried von
BESUCH DER ALTEN
  DAME
DANTONS TOD
PROZESS
ZERRISSENE

Ellis, Vivian
AND SO TO BED
BLESS THE BRIDE
JILL DARLING
MR. CINDERS (with R.
  Myers)

Ellstein, Abraham
GOLEM

Enesco, Georges
OEDIPUS

Engel, Lehman
MALADY OF LOVE
SOLDIER

Englander, Ludwig
BELLE OF BOHEMIA
  (with T. MacConnell)
CASINO GIRL
PASSING SHOW
RICH MR. HOGGENHEIM-
  ER
STROLLERS

Erlanger, Camille
APHRODITE
AUBE ROUGE

Erlanger, Frederic D'
TESS

Eysler, Edmund
BRUDER STRAUBINGER
GOLDENE MEISTERIN

-F-

Fain, Sammy
CALAMITY JANE

Fall, Leo
DOLLAR PRINCENSSIN
GESCHIEDENE FRAU
LIEBE AUGUSTIN
MADAME POMPADOUR
ROSE VON STAMBUL

Falla, Manuel De
RETABLO DE MAESE
  PEDRO
VIDA BREVE

Faraday, Philip Michael
AMASIS, AN EGYPTIAN
  PRINCESS

Fauré, Gabriel
PENELOPE

Février Henri
FEMME NEU
GISMONDA
MONNA VANNA

Fink, Myron S.
JEREMIAH

Flagello, Nicholas
JUDGMENT OF ST.
  FRANCIS
SISTERS

Fletcher, Grant
CARRION CROW
SACK OF CALABASAS

Flotow, Friedrich Von
    ALESSANDRO STRA-
        DELLA
    MARTHA

Floyd, Carlisle
    FLOWER AND HAWK
    MARKHEIM
    OF MICE AND MEN
    PASSION OF JONATHAN
        WADE
    SLOW DUSK
    SUSANNAH
    WUTHERING HEIGHTS

Förster, Alban
    LORLE
    MAIDENS OF SCHILDA

Fomin, Yevstignei
    WIZARD MILLER, CHEAT
    AND MARRIAGE BROKER

Ford, Nancy
    LAST SWEET DAYS OF
        ISAAC

Forrest, George
    KISMET (Adapt. of music
        from PRINCE IGOR,
        Borodin, with R. Wright)

Fortner, Wolfgang
    BLUTHOCHZEIT

Foss, Lukas
    INTRODUCTIONS AND
        GOODBYES
    JUMPING FROG OF CA-
        LAVERAS COUNTY

Franchetti, Alberto
    CHRISTOFORO COLOMBO
    GERMANIA

Franchetti, Aldo
    NAMIKO-SAN

Fraser-Simson, Harold
    MAID OF THE MOUN-
        TAINS
    STREET SINGER

Friml, Rudolf
    FIREFLY
    HIGH JINKS
    KATINKA
    ROSE MARIE (with H.
        Stothart)
    SOMETIME
    THREE MUSKETEERS
    VAGABOND KING

Furst, William Wallace
    ISLE OF CHAMPAGNE

Fux, Johann
    COSTANZA E FORTEZ
    ZA

-G-

Ganne, Louis
    SALTIMBANQUES

Gardner, John
    MOON AND SIXPENCE
    VISITORS

Gatty, Nicholas Comyn
    DUKE OR DEVIL
    GREYSTEEL
    KING ALFRED AND
        THE CAKES
    PRINCE FERELON

Gavazzeni, Giandrea
    PAUL AND VIRGINIA

Gay, Noel
    ME AND MY GIRL

Gaynor, Charles
    LEND AN EAR

Godard, Benjamin
  VIVANDIERE

Goehr, Alexander
  ARDEN MUSS STERBEN
  NABOTH'S VINEYARD

Goetz, Hermann
  TAMING OF THE SHREW

Goldmark, Karl
  CRICKET ON THE
    HEARTH
  MERLIN
  QUEEN OF SHEBA

Gomez, Antonio Carlos
  GUARANY

Goodman, Alfred
  LADY IN ERMINE (with
    J. Gilbert)

Goossens, Eugene
  DON JUAN DE MAÑARA
  JUDITH

Gotovac, Jacov
  ERO THE JOKER

Gould, Morton
  BILLION DOLLAR BABY

Gounod, Charles Francois
  FAUST
  MEDECIN MALGRE LUI
  MIREILLE
  PHILEMON AND BAUCIS
  REINE DE SABA
  ROMEO ET JULIETTE

Grammann, Karl
  INGRID
  IRRLICHT
  MELUSINE

Granados y Campina, En-
  rique
  GOYESCAS

Grant, Percy
  TRIP TO CHINATOWN

Gray, Timothy
  HIGH SPIRITS (with H.
    Martin)

Grechaninov, Aleksandr
  DOBRINYA NIKITICH

Greene, Maurice
  FLORIMEL, OR LOVE'S
    REVENGE

Grétry, André
  DEUX AVARES
  MEPRISES PAR RES-
    SEMBLANCES
  RICHARD COEUR DE
    LION

Grieg, Edvard Hagerup
  SONG OF NORWAY
    (works of Grieg ad-
    apted by R. Wright
    & G. Forrest)

Grossman, Larry
  MINNIE'S BOYS

Grove, Isaac Van
  OTHER WISE MAN
  SHINING CHALICE

Grudeff, Marian
  BAKER STREET (with
    R. Jessel)

Gruenberg, Louis
  EMPEROR JONES
  JACK AND THE BEAN-
    STALK

Henze, Hans Werner
  BASSARIDS
  BOULEVARD SOLITUDE
  CIMARRON
  CUBANA, OR A LIFE
    FOR ART
  ELEGY FOR YOUNG
    LOVERS
  ENDE EINER WELT
  FLOSS DER MEDUSA
  JUNGE LORD
  KOENIG HIRSCH
  LANDARZT
  LANGWIERIGE WEG IN
    DIE WOHNUNG DER
    NATASCHA UNGEHEUR
  PRINZ VON HOMBURG
  WE COME TO THE RI-
    VER
  WUNDERTHEATER

Herbert, Victor
  BABES IN TOYLAND
  EILEEN
  FORTUNE TELLER
  IDOL'S EYE
  IT HAPPENED IN NORD-
    LAND
  MADELEINE
  MADEMOISELLE MO-
    DISTE
  NATOMA
  NAUGHTY MARIETTA
  ONLY GIRL
  PRINCESS 'PAT'
  RED MILL
  ROSE OF ALGERIA
  SERENADE
  SWEETHEARTS
  WIZARD OF THE
    NILE

Herman, Jerry
  HELLO, DOLLY!
  MAME
  MILK AND HONEY

Hérold, Louis J. F.
  PRE AUX CLERCS
  ZAMPA

Hervé, Florimond
  MAM'ZELLE NITOUCHE

Hester, Hal
  YOUR OWN THING
    (with D. Apolinar)

Heuberger, Richard
  OPERNBALL

Heusen, James Van
  SKYSCRAPER
  WALKING HAPPY

Hill, Richard
  CANTERBURY TALES

Hindemith, Paul
  CARDILLAC
  HIN UND ZURUECK
  LANGE WEIHNACHTS-
    MAHL
  LET'S BUILD A
    TOWN
  MATHIS DER MALER
  NEUES VOM TAGE

Hirsch, Louis A.
  GOING UP
  MARY

Hoddinott, Alun
  BEACH OF FALESA

Hoffmann, Max
  PARISIAN MODEL

Hoiby, Lee
  NATALIA PETROVNA
  SCARF
  SUMMER AND
    SMOKE

MY LADY MOLLY
SAN TOY

Jones, Stephen
POPPY

Joubert, John
PRISONER

-K-

Kabalevsky, Dmitrii
FAMILY OF TARAS

Kálmán, Emmerich
ARIZONA LADY
BAJADERE
CIRCUS PRINCESS
CZARDASFUERSTIN
FASCHINGSFEE
GRAEFIN MARIZA
HERZOGIN VON CHICAGO
HOLLANDWEIBCHEN
KAISERIN JOSEPHINE
SARI
TARTAJARAS

Kalmanoff, Martin
BALD PRIMA DONNA
GREAT STONE FACE
INSECT COMEDY
OPERA, OPERA
PHOTOGRAPH - 1920
VICTORY AT MASADA

Kander, John
CABARET
FAMILY AFFAIR
HAPPY TIME
ZORBA

Kanitz, Ernest
KUMANA
LUCKY DOLLAR
PERPETUAL
ROOM NO. 12
ROYAL AUCTION

Karr, Harold
HAPPY HUNTING

Kaskel, Karl Von
HOCHZEITSMORGEN

Kastle, Leonard
DESERET

Kauer, Ferdinand
LESTA, THE DNIEPER
SPRITE

Kay, Ulysses
BOOR
CAPITOLINE VENUS
JUGGLER OF OUR
LADY

Kechley, Gerald
GOLDEN LION

Keiser, Reinhard
MASANIELLO FURIOSO

Kelemen, Milko
BELAGERUNGZUSTAND

Kenward, Elmslie
LIZZIE BORDEN

Kern, Jerome
CAT AND THE FIDDLE
CRISS CROSS
GOOD MORNING
DEARIE
LEAVE IT TO JANE
MUSIC IN THE AIR
OH BOY!
ROBERTA
SALLY
SHOW BOAT
STEPPING STONES
SUNNY
SWEET ADELINE
VERY GOOD, EDDIE

Kerker, Gustave
  BELLE OF NEW YORK
  CASTLES IN THE AIR
  CHINESE HONEYMOON
    (with H. Talbot)
  SOCIAL WHIRL

Kienzl, Wilhelm
  EVANGELIMANN
  KUHREIGEN
  URVASI

Killmayer, Wilhelm
  BUFFONATA
  YOLIMBA, ODER DIE
    GRENZEN DER MAGIE

Klebe, Giselher
  TOEDLICHEN WUENSCHE

Klenau, Paul Von
  MICHAEL KOHLHASS
  REMBRANDT VAN RIJN

Kodály, Zoltán
  HARY JANOS

Kohs, Ellis B.
  AMERIKA

Kollo, Walter
  FRAU OHNE KUSS

Korngold, Erich
  TOTE STADT
  VIOLANTE

Koval, Marian V.
  EMEL'YAN PUGACHOV

Koven, Reginald De
  CANTERBURY PILGRIMS
  HIGHWAYMAN
  MAID MARIAN
  RIP VAN WINKLE
  ROB ROY
  ROBIN HOOD

Kreisler, Fritz
  APPLE BLOSSOMS
  SISSY

Křenek, Ernst
  BELL TOWER
  DARK WATERS
  JONNY SPIELT AUF
  ORESTES
  WHAT PRICE CONFI-
    DENCE

Kretschmer, Edmund
  FOLKUNGER
  HENRY THE LION

Kreutz, Arthur
  SOURWOOD MOUNTAIN

Kreutzer, Konradin
  NACHTLAGER VON
    GRANADA

Křička, Jaroslav
  SPUK IM SCHLOSS

Kubelik, Rafael
  CORNELIA FAROLI

Künneke, Eduard
  DORF OHNE GLOCKE
  GLUECKLICHE REISE
  VETTER AUS DINGSDA
  WENN LIEBE ERWACHT

Kupferman, Meyer
  IN A GARDEN

Kurka, Robert
  GOOD SOLDIER
    SCHWEIK

-L-

Lacome, Paul
  MA MIE ROSETTE

CLEOPATRA
REINE FIAMETTA

Lesur, Daniel
ANDREA DEL SARTO

Levy, Harold
LOVELY LADY (with D.
Stamper)

Levy, Marvin David
ESCORIAL
MOURNING BECOMES
ELECTRA
SOTOBA KOMACHI
TOWER

Liebermann, Rolf
PENELOPE
SCHOOL FOR WIVES

Lindner, Eugen
MASTER THIEF

Link, Peter
SALVATION (with C.
Courtney)

Lincke, Paul
FRAU LUNA

Liszt, Franz
LEGENDE VON DER
HEILIGEN ELISABETH

Lloyd, George
IERNIN
JOHN SOCMAN
SERF

Lockwood, Normand
HANGING JUDGE
SCARECROW
WIZARDS OF BALIZAR

Loesser, Frank
GUYS AND DOLLS

HOW TO SUCCEED IN
BUSINESS WITHOUT
REALLY TRYING
MOST HAPPY FELLA
WHERE'S CHARLEY?

Loewe, Frederick
BRIGADOON
CAMELOT
DAY BEFORE SPRING
MY FAIR LADY
PAINT YOUR WAGON

London, Edwin
TALA OBTUSITIES

Lortzing, Gustav Albert
TWO GRENADIERS
UNDINE
WAFFENSCHMIED
WILDSCHUETZ
ZAR UND ZIMMERMANN

Luders, Gustav
BURGOMASTER
FAIR CO-ED
KING DODO
PRINCE OF PILSEN
SHO-GUN
WOODLAND

Lully, Jean Baptiste
ALCESTA

Lutyens, Elisabeth
INFIDELIO
TIME OFF? NOT A
GHOST OF A CHANCE!

Lyford, Ralph
CASTLE AGRAZANT

-M-

MacConnell, T.
BELLE OF BOHEMIA
(with L. Englander)

SERAGLIO
BASTIEN AND BASTIENNE
CLEMENZA DI TITO
COSI FAN TUTTE
DON GIOVANNI
FINTA GIARDINIERA
FINTA SEMPLICE
IDOMENEO
LUCIO SILLA
MAGIC FLUTE
MITRIDATE
NOZZE DI FIGARO
OCA DEL CAIRO
RE PASTORE
SCHAUSPIELDIREKTOR

Mulè, Giuseppe
LIOLA

Murphy, Owen
RAIN OR SHINE (with M.
Ager)

Musgrave, Thea
DECISION
VOICE OF ARIADNE

Musorgskii, Modest
BORIS GODOUNOV
FAIR AT SOROCHINTZKY
KHOVANSHCHINA
MARRIAGE

Myers, Richard
MISTER CINDERS (with
V. Ellis)

-N-

Napravnik, Edward F.
DUBROVSKY

Nedbal, Oskar
POLENBLUT

Nessler, Victor E.
PIPER OF HAMELIN
TRUMPETER OF SAEK-
KINGEN

Nicolai, Otto
MERRY WIVES OF
WINDSOR

Nielsen, Carl
MASKARADE
SAUL AND DAVID

Norton, Frederic
CHU CHIN CHOW

Nouguès, Jean
QUO VADIS

Novello, Ivor
DANCING YEARS
GLAMOROUS NIGHT
KING'S RHAPSODY
PERCHANCE TO DREAM

-O-

Offenbach, Jacques
BA-TA-CLAN
BARBE-BLEUE
BELLE HELENE
BRIGANDS
CHANSON DE FORTUNIO
CHRISTOPHER COLUM-
BUS (music by Don
White & Lorraine
Thomas. Orig. La
Boite Au Lait)
DEMOISELLE EN LO-
TERIE
FILLE DU TAMBOUR-
MAJOR
GOLDSCHMIED VON
TOLEDO
GRAND DUCHESS OF
GIROLSTEIN

152   Composer Index

Puccini, Giacomo
BOHEME
FANCIULLA DEL WEST
GIANNI SCHICCHI
MADAME BUTTERFLY
MANON LESCAUT
RONDINE
SUOR ANGELICA
TABARRO
TOSCA
TURANDOT
VILLI

Purcell, Daniel
JUDGMENT OF PARIS

Purcell, Henry
DIDO AND AENEAS
FAIRY QUEEN
KING ARTHUR

-R-

Rabaud, Henry
MÂROUF, LE SAVETIER
DU CAIRE
ROLANDE ET LE MAU-
VAIS GARÇON

Rachmaninoff, Sergei
ALEKO
FRANCESCA DA RIMINI
MISERLY KNIGHT

Rameau, Jean Philippe
ABARIS, OU LES BO-
READES
CASTOR AND POLLUX
DARDANUS
FÊTES D'HEBE

Ramsier, Paul
MAN ON THE BEARSKIN
RUG

Rankl, Karl
DEIRDRE OF THE SOR-
ROWS

Ravel, Maurice
ENFANT ET LES SOR-
TILEGES
HEURE ESPAGNOLE

Refice, Licinio
CECILIA

Reimann, Aribert
MELUSINE

Reinecke, Carl
BY ORDER OF HIS
HIGHNESS

Respighi, Ottorino
FIAMMA
LUCREZIA
MARIA EGIZIACA
SUNKEN BELL

Reutter, Herman
DR. JOHANNES FAUST

Reyer, Ernest
SALAMMBO
SIGURD

Reynolds, Alfred
DERBY DAY

Reznicek, Emil Nikolaus von
DONNA DIANA

Rheinhardt, Heinrich
SUESSE MAEDEL

Ricci, Ferderico
CRISPINO E LA CO-
MARE (with L. Ricci)

Ricci, Luigi
CRISPINO E LA CO-
MARE (with F. Ricci)

Rice, E. E.
  EVANGELINE

Rieti, Vittorio
  CLOCK
  DON PERLIMPLIN
  PET SHOP

Rimskii-Korsakov, Nikolai
  COQ D'OR
  KASHCHEY THE IMMOR-
    TAL
  KITEZH
  LEGEND OF TSAR SUL-
    TAN
  MAY NIGHT
  MOZART AND SALIERI
  PSKOVITYANKA
  SADKO
  SNEGOUROCHKA
  TSAR'S BRIDE

Ritter, Alexander
  IDLE HANS

Rocca, Lodovico
  DYBBUK

Rodgers, Mary
  ONCE UPON A MATTRESS

Rodgers, Richard
  ALLEGRO
  AMERICA'S SWEET-
    HEART
  BABES IN ARMS
  BOYS FROM SYRACUSE
  BY JUPITER
  CAROUSEL
  CONNECTICUT YANKEE
  DEAREST ENEMY
  DO I HEAR A WALTZ?
  FLOWER-DRUM SONG
  GIRL FRIEND
  I MARRIED AN ANGEL
  I'D RATHER BE RIGHT
  JUMBO

KING AND I
ME AND JULIET
NO STRINGS
OKLAHOMA
ON YOUR TOES
PAL JOEY
PEGGY-ANN
PIPE DREAM
PRESENT ARMS
SIMPLE SIMON
SOUND OF MUSIC
SOUTH PACIFIC

Rogers, Bernard
  NIGHTINGALE
  VEIL
  WARRIOR

Romberg, Sigmund
  ARTISTS AND MODELS
    (with J. Coots)
  BLOSSOM TIME
  BLUE PARADISE
  BOMBO
  DESERT SONG
  GIRL IN PINK TIGHTS
  INNOCENT EYES
  MY MARYLAND
  MAY WINE
  MAYTIME
  NEW MOON
  ROBINSON CRUSOE, JR.
  SINBAD
  STUDENT PRINCE
  UP IN CENTRAL PARK

Rome, Harold
  CALL ME MISTER
  DESTRY RIDES AGAIN
  FANNY
  I CAN GET IT FOR
    YOU WHOLESALE
  WISH YOU WERE HERE

Rorem, Ned
  BERTHA
  CHILDHOOD MIRACLE

FABLES
MISS JULIE
ROBBERS
THREE SISTERS WHO
  WERE NOT SISTERS

Rosenthal, Manuel
  POULE NOIRE

Ross, Jerry
  DAMN YANKEES (with R.
    Adler)
  PAJAMA GAME (with R.
    Adler)

Rossini, Gioacchino
  ASSEDIO DI CORINTO
  BARBIERE DI SEVIGLIA
  CAMBIALE DI MATRIMO-
    NIO
  CENERENTOLA
  COMTE ORY
  DONNA DEL LAGO
  ELIZABETH, QUEEN OF
    ENGLAND
  GAZZA LADRA
  ITALIANA IN ALGERI
  MOISE (revision of MOSE
    IN EGITTO)
  MOSE IN EGITTO
  PIETRA DEL PARAGONE
  SEMIRAMIDE
  SIGNOR BRUSCHINO
  TANCREDI
  TURCO IN ITALIA
  WILLIAM TELL

Rousseau, Jean-Jacques
  DEVIN DU VILLAGE

Roussel, Albert
  AUNT CAROLINE'S WILL
  PADMAVATI

Roy, Klaus George
  STERLINGMANN, OR,
    GENEROSITY REWARD

Rubens, Paul
  GIRL FROM UTAH
  LADY MADCAP
  MISS HOOK OF HOL-
    LAND
  SUNSHINE GIRL

Rubinstein, Anton
  DEMON
  MACCABEES
  NERO

Ruby, Harry
  ANIMAL CRACKERS
  FIVE O'CLOCK GIRL
  GOOD BOY (with H.
    Stothart)
  HELEN OF TROY, NEW
    YORK
  RAMBLERS

-S-

Saint-Saëns, Camille
  DEJANIRE
  HELENE
  HENRY VIII
  SAMSON AND DELILA

Salieri, Antonio
  LITTLE HARLEQUINADE
  PRIMA LA MUSICA, POI
    LE PAROLE

Salsbury, Nate
  BROOK

Sanders, Carlo
  TANGERINE

Sandrich, Mark, Jr.
  BEN FRANKLIN IN
    PARIS

Scarlatti, Alessandro
  EQUIVOCI IN AMORE

Smetana, Bedřich
BARTERED BRIDE
BRANDENBURGERS IN
BOHEMIA
DALIBOR
DEVIL'S WALL
DVE VDOVY
KISS
LIBUSE
SECRET

Smyth, Ethel
BOATSWAIN'S MATE
FÊTE GALANTE
FOREST
WRECKERS

Sokoloff, Noel
FRANKLIN'S TALE
PARDONER'S TALE

Solomon, Edward
BILLEE TAYLOR
NAUTCH GIRL OR THE
RAJAH OF CHUTNEY-
PORE
VICAR OF BRAY

Somerville, Reginald
MOUNTAINEERS

Sondheim, Stephan
ANYONE CAN WHISTLE
COMPANY
FUNNY THING HAP-
PENED ON THE WAY
TO THE FORUM

Sousa, John Philip
AMERICAN MAID
BRIDE-ELECT
CAPITAN
CHARLATAN
CHRIS AND THE WON-
DERFUL LAMP
DESIREE
FREE LANCE

QUEEN OF HEARTS
SMUGGLERS
WOLF

Spencer, Willard
LITTLE TYCOON
PRINCESS BONNIE

Spinelli, Nicola
A BASSO PORTO

Spohr, Louis
JESSONDA

Spontini, Gasparo
VESTALE
PETITE MAISON

Stambler, Bernard
SERVANT OF TWO
MASTERS

Stamper, Dave
LOVELY LADY (with
H. Levy)
TAKE THE AIR

Stanford, Charles Villiers
CRITIC
MUCH ADO ABOUT
NOTHING
SHAMUS O'BRIEN
TRAVELLING COM-
PANION

Starer, Robert
PANTAGLEIZE

Still, William
TROUBLED ISLAND

Stoessel, Albert
GARRICK

Stokes, Eric
HORSPFAL

-Z-

Zandonai, Riccardo
    CONCHITA
    FARSA AMOROSA
    FRANCESCA DA RIMINI

Zeller, Karl
    OBERSTEIGER
    VOGELHAENDLER

Ziehrer, Karl
    LANDESTREICHER

Zimbalist, Efrem
    HONEYDEW

Zimmerman, Alois
    SOLDATEN

PART IV

Bibliography of Additional Sources

BIBLIOGRAPHY OF
ADDITIONAL SOURCES CONTAINING
OPERA, OPERETTA AND MUSICAL COMEDY SYNOPSES

Dictionaries and Encyclopedias

Ewen, David. Encyclopedia of the opera. New York: R. A. Wyn, 1955.

_____. The new encyclopedia of the opera. New York: Hill and Wang, 1971.

Moore, Frank Ledlie. Crowell's handbook of world opera. New York: Thomas Y. Crowell, 1961.

Orrey, Leslie, ed. The encyclopedia of opera. New York: Scribners, 1976.

Scholes, Percy Alfred. The Oxford companion to music. 10th ed. London: Oxford University Press, 1970.

Other Sources (Arranged alphabetically by composer)

BELLINI, VINCENZO

   Weinstock, Herbert. Vincenzo Bellini, his life and his operas. New York: A. A. Knopf, 1971.

BERNSTEIN, LEONARD

   Ewen, David. Leonard Bernstein, a biography for young people. Philadelphia: Chilton Co. , 1960.

BRITTEN, BENJAMIN

   Howard, Patricia. The operas of Benjamin Britten, an introduction. New York: Praeger, 1969.

Mitchell, Donald, and Keller, Hans, eds. Benjamin
Britten, a commentary on his works from a
group of specialists. New York: Philosophical
Library, 1952.

White, Eric Walter. Benjamin Britten, his life and
operas. Los Angeles: University of California
Press, 1970.

CHAIKOVSKII, PETR IL'ICH

Abraham, Gerald Ernest Heal, ed. The music of
Tchaikovsky. New York: W. W. Norton, 1946.
(Reissued 1969, Kennikat Press)

Warrack, John Hamilton. Tchaikovsky. London:
Hamish Hamilton, 1973.

CHERUBINI, LUIGI

Bellasis, Edward. Cherubini, memorials illustrative
of his life and work. New York: Da Capo Press,
1971. (original edition, 1912)

DEBUSSY, CLAUDE

Thompson, Oscar. Debussy, man and artist. New
York: Dodd, Mead and Co., 1937.

DELIUS, FREDERICK

Redwood, Christopher. A Delius companion. London:
John Calder, 1976.

DVORAK, ANTONIN

Fischl, Viktor, ed. Antonin Dvorak, his achievement.
Westport, Connecticut: Greenwood Press, 1970.
(Originally published 1943, London: Lindsay
Drummond)

EGK, WERNER

Krause, Ernst. Werner Egk, Oper und Ballet. Wil-
helmshaven: Heinrichshofen's Verlag, 1971. (In
German)

Bibliography   167

GERSHWIN, GEORGE

Schwartz, Charles. Gershwin, his life and mu-
    sic. Indianapolis: Bobbs-Merrill Company,
    1973.

GILBERT, SIR WILLIAM

Ayre, Leslie. The Gilbert and Sullivan compan-
    ion. New York: Dodd, Mead and Company,
    1972.

Harwick, Michael. The Osprey guide to Gilbert
    and Sullivan. Reading, England: Osprey,
    1972.

Kline, Peter. Gilbert and Sullivan productions. New
    York: Rosen Press, 1972.

Moore, Frank Ledlie, comp. Crowell's handbook of
    Gilbert and Sullivan. New York: Thomas Y.
    Crowell, 1962, 1975.

Williamson, Audrey. Gilbert and Sullivan opera.
    London: Salisbury Square, 1953.

GLINKA, MIKHAIL

Brown, David. Mikhail Glinka, a biographical and
    critical study. London: Oxford University Press,
    1974.

GOUNOD, CHARLES FRANCOIS

Harding, James. Gounod. London: George Allen &
    Unwin, 1973

HERBERT, VICTOR

Waters, Edward Neighbor. Victor Herbert, a life in
    music. New York: Macmillan, 1955.

JANACEK, LEOS

Chisholm, Erik. The operas of Leos Janacek. New
    York: Pergamon Press, 1971.

KRENEK, ERNST

Krenek, Ernst. Horizons circled, reflections on my
    music. Berkeley: University of California Press,
    1974.

Rogge, Wolfgang. Ernst Kreneks Opern, Spiegel der
    Zwanziger Jahre. Wolfenbuttel und Zurich:
    Moseler Verlag, 1970. (In German)

MARTINU, BOHUSLAV

Large, Brian. Martinu. London: Duckworth, 1975.

MASSENET, JULES

Finck, Henry Theophilus. Massenet and his operas.
    New York: John Lane, 1910. (Reprint 1976,
    AMS Press)

Irvine, Demar Buel. Massenet, a chronicle of his
    life and times. Seattle: The Author, 1974.

MONTEVERDI, CLAUDIO

Schrade, Leo. Monteverdi, creator of modern music.
    New York: W. W. Norton, 1950.

MOZART, WOLFGANG AMADEUS

Benn, Christopher. Mozart on the stage. London:
    Ernest Benn, 1946.

Dent, Edward Joseph. Mozart's operas, critical study.
    2nd ed. London: Oxford University Press,
    1947.

Hughes, Spike [Patrick Cairns]. Famous Mozart opera,
    an analytical guide for the opera goer and arm-
    chair listener. 2nd ed. New York: Dover,
    1972, 1958.

MUSORGSKII, MODEST

Calvocoressi, Michel D. Mussorgsky. London: J.
    M. Dent, 1974.

PUCCINI, GIACOMO

    Ashbrook, William. The operas of Puccini. New
        York: Oxford University Press, 1968.

    Hughes, Spike [Patrick Cairns]. Famous Puccini op-
        eras, an analytical guide for the opera goer and
        armchair listener. 2nd ed. New York: Dover,
        1972, 1959.

    Macdonald, Ray S. Puccini, king of verismo. New
        York: Vantage Press, 1973.

RAMEAU, JEAN PHILIPPE

    Girdlestone, Cuthbert Morton. Jean-Philippe Rameau,
        his life and work. London: Cassell, 1957.
        (Rev. ed. , 1969, Dover Press)

ROSSINI, GIOACCHINO

    Stendhal, pseud. [Beyle, Marie Henri]. Life of Ros-
        sini. Trans. Richard N. Coe. New York: Cri-
        terion Books, 1957.

SAINT-SAENS, CAMILLE

    Hervey, Arthur. Saint-Saens. New York: Books for
        Libraries Press, 1969

SMETANA, BEDRICH

    Clapham, John. Smetana. London: J. M. Dent;
        New York: Octagon Books, 1972.

STRAUSS, RICHARD

    Lehmann, Lotte. Five operas and Richard Strauss.
        Trans. Ernst Pawel. New York: Macmillan, 1964.

    Mann, William S. Richard Strauss, a critical study
        of the operas. New York: Oxford University
        Press, 1966.

STRAVINSKY, IGOR

    White, Eric Walter. Stravinsky, the composer and his

works. Los Angeles: University of California
Press, 1966.

VAUGHAN WILLIAMS, RALPH

Kennedy, Michael. The works of Ralph Vaughan Williams. London: Oxford University Press, 1964.

VERDI, GIUSEPPE

Budden, Julian. The operas of Verdi, I: From Ober-
to to Rigoletto. London: Cassell, 1973.

Godefroy, Vincent. The dramatic genius of Verdi,
studies of selected operas; Vol. I. London:
Gollancz, 1975.

Hughes, Spike [Patrick Cairns]. Famous Verdi operas,
an analytical guide for the opera goer and arm-
chair listener. Philadelphia: Chilton Book Co.,
1968.

Osborne, Charles. Complete operas of Verdi. New
York: A. A. Knopf, 1970.

Toye, Francis. Giuseppe Verdi, his life and works.
New York: Vienna House, 1972.

Williams, Stephen. Verdi's last operas. London:
Hinrichsen Edition, 1950.

WAGNER, RICHARD

Buesst, Aylmer. The Nibelung's ring, an act-by-act
guide to the plot and music. London: Newman
Neame [n. d.]

Guerber, Helene Adelina. Stories of the Wagner opera.
New York: Dodd, Mead, 1898.

Kobbe, Gustav. Wagner's music-dramas analyzed, with
the leading motives. New York: G. Schirmer, 1904.

Lavignac, Albert. The music dramas of Richard Wagner and his festival theatre in Bayreuth. New
York: AMS Press, 1970. (Original edition,
1904)

Newman, Ernest. The Wagner operas. New York:
     A. A. Knopf, 1949.

Weston, Jessie Laidley. The legends of the Wagner
     drama; studies in mythology and romances. New
     York: Scribner's, 1896.